# THE
# SQUARE ROOT
# OF TUESDAY

# THE
# SQUARE ROOT
# OF TUESDAY

*Jessica Davidson*

E. P. Dutton & Co., Inc.   New York

Published simultaneously in Canada by Clarke,
Irwin & Company Limited, Toronto and Vancouver

SBN: 0-525-39850-3    LCC: 73-135445

Printed in the U.S.A.
Second Printing, June 1974

For *A. Harris Stone,*
who can extract the square root of Tuesday as easily as he can fit twenty-seven hours into any day

# Contents

# THE
# SQUARE ROOT
# OF TUESDAY

# 0

# *Introduction*

Teenagers have too much freedom.

The only requirement for admission to a movie should be having the price of a ticket.

End the war in Vietnam.

The army builds men.

Smoking marijuana should not be illegal.

Most of today's crimes can be traced to the use of drugs.

Guns should be outlawed.

Abolish report cards.

Automobile manufacturers should be forced to include safety features in their cars.

Win the war in Vietnam at all costs.

Every student should be required to salute the flag.

Parents should be held responsible for their children's conduct.

Student protesters who disrupt the school program should be expelled.

Rock music festivals should be banned.

Surely there must have been at least one statement among those listed above with which you agree or disagree strongly. How do you convince someone of a point of view you agree with? How do you argue effectively against a conclusion with which you disagree?

That is what this book is mostly about. It might have been called "How to Win an Argument" or at least "How Not to Lose an Argument." The first few chapters are about formal logic, about how to discover whether a conclusion necessarily follows from the premises—the ideas or information—which claim to support it. They are concerned with discovering what conclusions *can* be drawn from the facts or ideas you have agreed to accept as true. They will show you how to build up arguments and how to tear them down. They will show you how to construct traps and how not to get caught in them. If you do get caught in them, you'll find some advice about how to crawl out without bleeding too much.

Logic doesn't solve problems. It provides a framework, an orderly system, for stating the problem and seeking a solution. Blueprints don't build houses, but better houses are built with the use of them. Logic is not a method for finding the truth of anything. Just as owning a pair of well-fitting shoes will not teach a baby to walk, so logic will not teach you to think. You will have to look elsewhere for truth. This book is not about truth. The truth of a conclusion depends on the truth of the premises and not merely on whether the argument is in correct form. You will have to look elsewhere for the facts as to whether cigarette smoking is hazardous to your health. This book will help you only to draw some conclusions as to what should be done about it, if it is, and how to convince others of your point of view about it.

This book will also deal with the question of who should make the decisions, you or a computer. And, after giving you a little look at how the mind works, or should work, it will touch very briefly on the question of when you should let your rational mind alone and do a little feeling about a subject.

Formal logic has as strict a structure as mathematics. That makes it very hard to begin in the middle. This is too bad, because the beginning of a subject is often very dull; the middle is more interesting. Many an author of a book on logic wonders whether the beginning is going to be so dull that no one will get through it to the middle. Perhaps that is why most books on logic are textbooks. That way, the author can be sure that some teacher will force his readers to get to the middle. It would be pleasant to begin in the middle, but if you were asked to explain to someone how to multiply 493 by 207, could you do it before making sure that he knew what was meant by the zero in 207? And if he said, "Oh, I know what zero is. Zero is nothing," would that help you? So, if you start to skip some of the material in the first couple of chapters because you think you know it already, please be sure that you're not one of those people who doesn't have to find out about zero because zero is nothing.

# 1

# *Boxed-in Thinking*

On the opposite page there is a picture of the universe. The reason you can't see anything there is that the picture is drawn to scale. Below is a picture of a different kind of universe. It is not drawn to any scale whatever, nor does it exist, except in the mind. Its formal name is "the universe of discourse." Translated, this means everything we happen to be talking about right now. The universe of discourse for this picture is "living creatures."

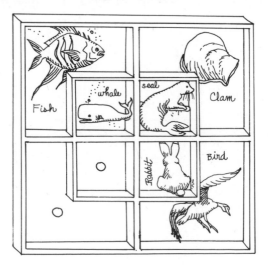

For this particular picture, the universe of discourse has been divided into compartments. All of the upper half is for water creatures, the lower half for all other creatures. All of the left-hand side is for creatures with fins; those without fins go on the right. The center square is for mammals and the rest of the large square is for creatures that are not mammals.

A representative creature, if there is one, has been drawn in each compartment. The fish belongs in the upper half because it is a water creature. It belongs on the left because it has fins. It is outside the inner square because it is not a mammal. The whale is also on the upper left because it is a water creature with fins, but it is within the inner square because it is a mammal. Check to see that the seal, the clam, the rabbit and the bird are properly placed. Two compartments are empty, marked *O* for zero, because there are no creatures with fins (whether mammals or not) that are not water animals.

Since drawing pictures is difficult for some people and, in any case, takes a lot of time, this game of logic is better played with diagrams. This is what the diagram would look like:

The *I* means that there is at least one creature that belongs in the compartment and the *O* means that there are none.

Diagrams like this are rather hard to follow until you get the hang of them, so let's go back to the beginning, start slowly, and find out how to get to this point and beyond. What are we aiming for? Why bother? Well, let's look at a few sample arguments:

> If cats are mammals and if all mammals are animals, then a cat is an animal.

Agreed?

> No fish are mammals and no birds are fish, so no birds are mammals.

Is the argument correct? Then how about this one, in exactly the same form:

> No fish are mammals and no cats are fish, so no cats are mammals.

Do you think it's false? Could you prove it? Is it enough to say you just *know* the conclusion isn't true?

Probably you just know that 50 percent of six is three, but since you probably don't "just know" what 37 percent of 456 is, you have to find out how to go about it. In the same way, if you want to play the logic game, you have to learn the rules and practice using them, and it's easier to begin with simple examples. That's why we're going to bother.

Here is an empty bookcase. It is going to contain "the universe of books that a family is unpacking."

The family has just moved to a new house. The boxes of books have been unpacked and books are strewn all over the floor. It is your job to get them off the floor and into the case but, to help in organizing them, you are to follow these rules: Children's books go in the left-hand section of the bookcase, adult books in the right-hand section. All tall books go on the top shelf and those that are not tall go on the bottom shelf.

You plunge right into the job. Here's *Winnie-the-Pooh,* a small book. Put it on the lower left. Here's *The Silver Book of Astronomy,* a tall book—upper left. Here's a volume of Shakespeare, tall. It goes on the upper right. Poems by John Milton, not tall—lower right. And so the task goes on.

But here's a problem: *The World Atlas.* It's tall, so it has to go on the upper shelf, but does it belong on the children's side or the adults'? Both use it. Well, fortunately, the bookcase has that odd section right in the middle of the top shelf. Put it there, just for now, till you decide whether it should go on the right or the left.

Here's another problem, the "What You Want to Know About" series. They're all children's books, but some are tall and others aren't. You *could* split them up on the two left-hand shelves, but perhaps they ought to be kept together as a series. Until you decide, there's another convenient halfway spot. Lay them flat in the space between the upper and lower shelves on the left.

Because it's tiresome to keep on drawing bookcases, will you settle for a diagram? And because it's unimportant, under the rules, whether there is one book or a hundred on a given shelf, will you agree that if there are *any* books that belong in a shelf, we'll mark that shelf with an *I* to show it's not empty. If there are no books at all for a given shelf we'll mark the space with a *O,* and if we don't know whether any books belong on the shelf or not, we'll leave the space blank.

Here are some diagrams with explanations:

 There are tall books, some for children, some for adults.

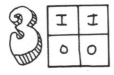 All the children's books are tall, but there are some tall books that are not for children.

 All the books are tall; some are for children, some for adults.

 All the tall books are for children. No adult books are tall. All the not-tall books are for adults. There are some tall books and some not-tall books.

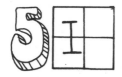 There are some children's books, maybe they're tall, maybe they're not tall, maybe both.

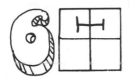 There are some tall books, maybe for children, maybe for adults, maybe for both.

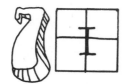 There are some books, but it's not decided yet whether they're tall or not, nor whether they're for children or for adults or both.

Before going any further, it is important to notice what these diagrams *do not* say. Diagram 1 does not say whether there are any short books for children, or any short books for adults or any short books at all. If we knew that there were no short books, there would be a *O* in each of the lower spaces. The squares are blank, and this indicates "no information." But diagram 1 can also represent the statement "Not all tall books are for children" and "Some tall books are not for adults" and similar variations on the same theme.

Diagram 5 does not say that there are no adult books. Diagram 6 does not say that there are no short books.

Consider this diagram. What do you think it says? Certainly it says "There are no tall children's books." That much is clear. Does it also say "All children's books are not tall"? Yes, in a way it says that, but be careful, because it does not say that there *are* any children's books at all. The most precise information you can get from this diagram is "If there are any children's books, they're not tall" or "If there are any tall books, they're not for children."

Since we've abandoned the bookcase for the diagram, we're not limited to the universe of books. Let's try the universe of people. Some people are redheaded and some aren't. Put the redheaded people on the left. Everybody else on the right. Some people are good spellers. Put them in the top half of the diagram. Those who aren't must go on the bottom.

This yields: There are some good spellers who don't have red hair.

Too much of the book's space is being used for diagrams. Go get your own paper. Can you diagram each of these?

1. Some poor spellers have red hair.
2. All good spellers have red hair.
3. There are no poor spellers.
4. Some people are good spellers.
5. Some poor spellers have red hair and some don't.
6. No poor spellers have red hair.
7. No redheads are poor spellers.

If you want to check your answers, look at the end of the chapter. (But, of course, you can't check your answers if you haven't got any.)

Try now to find your own labels for the squares. You might practice with these:

8. Some teachers are not intelligent.
9. There are many students, but there is no such person as a student who is never bored.
10. All cats have whiskers, and cats exist.
11. If there are any unicorns, they have a single horn.
12. People who like chocolate sauce on pickles are crazy.

You will find these diagrams at the end of the chapter, too, in case you're not feeling self-confident.

Sometimes it's hard to tell exactly what a statement means. For instance, to "all cats have whiskers," we added "and cats exist." This seems pretty obvious, because everyone knows there are cats, so why bother to put it down? "All unicorns have a single horn" has the same grammatical form, but you know that unicorns don't exist. Suppose you don't know, one way or the other, as in the case of "people who like chocolate sauce on pickles." The best rule is to leave a square blank unless you have definite information that there are or are not examples that belong in it. If the premises state that cats exist you can put an *I* in the whiskered cat box. Otherwise, you can only put a *O* in the unwhiskered cat box. That's why you should diagram "People who live in glass houses shouldn't throw stones" this way:

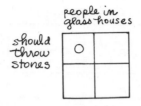

One of the advantages of using the boxes to state an argument is that you have to know precisely what you mean before you can fill the boxes properly. Suppose you get into an argument about Romeo's famous statement, "He jests at scars that never felt a wound." Do you agree or disagree? Either way, let's try to put the statement into the boxes. Reserve the top half of the diagram for the jokers, those who jest at scars. The bottom's for the non-jokers. On the left put the wounded, on the right, those who never felt a wound. Which of the following diagrams correctly shows what Romeo had in mind?

Romeo's not available to answer, but if you're arguing about the truth of his statement, it's a good idea to decide what you think it means. People often say things like "Italians are emotional." How would you diagram it? All Italians? Some Italians? Only Italians? "Geniuses are temperamental," "Politicians are crooks," and "Poetry can't be translated" present similar problems.

To work up to the diagram at the beginning of this chapter, start with the universe of mammals and set up the boxes this way:

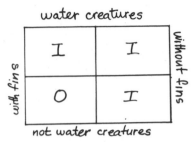

This diagram says, "There are some water mammals with fins and some without." It also says, "Only water creatures have fins" and "Mammals without fins may be water creatures or not."

So far, the diagram says nothing about creatures that are not mammals. To bring in such creatures we need to enlarge our universe. We do this by drawing a larger area around the diagram.

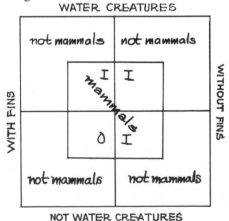

Everything in the inner square—the one we've been using for mammals—remains the same. Everything outside the inner square is now available for creatures that are not mammals. But in all other ways the rules remain the same. Everything on the top half, of both the inner and the outer squares, is a water creature. Everything on the left of the center line, in the small square and the large one, has fins; nothing on the right side does. We do not have to change any of the information that is already in the boxes. We need only consider what symbols, if any, to place in the four new spaces. On the upper left, for water creatures with fins that are not mammals, we put an *I* because there are fish. An *I* goes in the upper right for water creatures with no fins, who are not mammals, such as clams. A *O* goes on the bottom left, to show that there are no creatures that can be described as not mammals, not water creatures, but with fins. An *I* goes on the lower right because there are birds who are not mammals, are not water creatures, and have no fins.

The particular boxes we have been using were created by Lewis Carroll, who is best known as the author of *Alice in Wonderland,* but who was also a mathematician. He was one of the first to set up a system of diagrams for symbolic logic, a method of using symbols rather than words to show how arguments can be built and checked for correct reasoning. The pioneer of symbolic logic was the nineteenth century English mathematician, George Boole. Another nineteenth century English mathematician, John Venn, invented the diagrams that are most commonly used in symbolic logic today. You may have met Venn diagrams in your math classes, where they are used to show operations on sets. They're equally useful in showing logical relations.

The Venn diagrams that will be used here are in the form of overlapping circles. Sections of the circles that are empty are shaded in or scratched out, as if they were erased. (You will find some logic books that do exactly the opposite—they shade in the *occupied* spaces. But Venn himself did it the way we're doing it here and it's more convenient, because it's hard to see, when a section is shaded in, whether or not it has a symbol in it.) Sections that are occupied are marked with a bar, but we shall use the same *I* we've used in the boxes, and it will mean the same thing. Sections that have neither a bar nor shading are sections about which we have no information, as in the boxes.

To use the Venn diagrams to show information about children's books and tall books we would use two over-lapping circles:

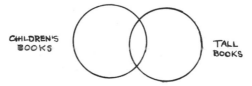

The section where the circles overlap represents children's books that are tall. If the section is shaded, there are no tall children's books:

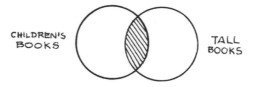

If the section has a bar (an *I*) in it, there are some tall children's books:

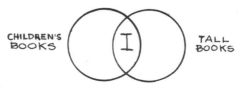

If the section is left blank, there is no information as to whether there are any tall children's books or not.

The sections of the circles that do not overlap are equally important. A shaded section is empty. Thus this diagram shows that there are no children's books that are *not* tall:

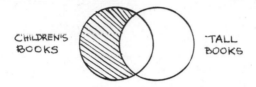

It's useful to know how to use both the boxes and the Venn diagrams, as you will see later on, and it's not hard to translate from one to the other.

Both diagrams show the statement "Some children's books are tall":

These diagrams show "All children's books are tall," if you mean that if there *are* any children's books, they're tall:

(Empty sections—the section for children's books that are not tall—are shaded.)

These diagrams show "All children's books are tall and there are some children's books":

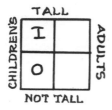 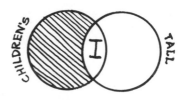

Here are the diagrams for "No children's books are tall":

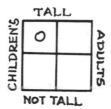 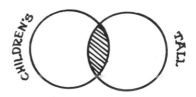

and for "Some children's books are not tall":

 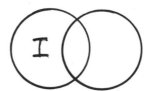

In the Venn diagrams, as in the boxes, you can have a bar that sits on the fence. Here are the diagrams for "There are some children's books but there's no information as to whether they're tall or not":

 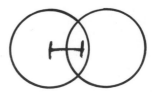

To match the boxes that we used for the universe of

living creatures, Venn used three interlocking circles like those in the beer trademark:

These three rings provide seven sections, as the numbers show. Section 1 is the area where all three circles overlap. Sections 2, 3, and 4 are areas where two of the three circles overlap. Sections 5, 6, and 7 are areas of single circles.

Interpreting the diagram to discover whether a creature is a mammal or not, has fins or not, or is a water creature or not, we label the three rings and identify the seven areas in the following way:

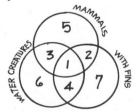

Notice the position of the circle for mammals. It is the top circle, added afterwards, just as the space used to set apart mammals and not mammals was added afterwards around the basic four boxes. The occupants of the circle sections are, then, these:

1. water mammals with fins—whales
2. mammals with fins who are not water creatures—empty
3. mammals who are water creatures and have no fins—seals
4. water creatures with fins who are not mammals—fish
5. mammals who have no fins and are not water creatures—rabbits
6. water creatures who have no fins and are not mammals—clams
7. creatures with fins who are not mammals or water creatures—empty

Do you notice that one of our creatures is missing? In Venn diagrams, the birds, who are not mammals, are not water creatures, and have no fins, have no place to roost, but must simply fly around freely in the universe of discourse outside the circles.

Lewis Carroll's boxes thus offer a more complete method of showing the universe of creatures (or any other universe of discourse). They also have the advantage of showing more clearly that if some teachers are not intelligent, then some unintelligent people are teachers, while the Venn diagrams do not, at first, seem to say anything about unintelligent people:

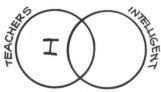

In using the Venn diagrams you have to be careful not to miss some of the possible meanings of the circles, finding only one conclusion when there are several. But the Venn diagrams are much easier to label and they are commonly used in the logic textbooks today in solving questions of proof. That is why we shall use them most of the time in the next chapters, bringing in the boxes only occasionally for comparison. But you may take your choice.

## ANSWERS

These are the redheaded spellers diagrams. Good spellers across the top, redheads on the left.

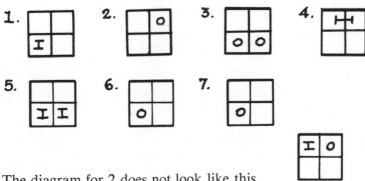

The diagram for 2 does not look like this because no information is given about whether there are any good spellers at all. Diagrams 6 and 7 are the same because if no redheads are poor spellers then there are no poor spellers who have red hair.

8. teachers     9. students     10. cats

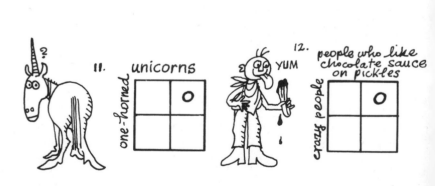

11. unicorns     12. people who like chocolate sauce on pickles

# 2

# *Going Around in Circles*

Comparing his last name with those of two of his friends, George discovered the following:

Some letters in Susan's name were also in his. All the letters in his name were also in Kim's.

Do Kim's last name and Susan's necessarily have any letters in common?

The Venn diagrams can answer the question. Since George's name is the one with which both Susan's and Kim's are being compared, it should be given the middle circle, the one on top, like this:

The first information to record is that all the letters in George's name are also in Kim's. This means that the section of George's circle which doesn't overlap Kim's must be empty, so it should be shaded:

The next fact to record is that some of the letters in Susan's name are also in George's. Since part of the overlap between George's circle and Susan's is already shaded to show that it's empty, there's only one spot left to put the bar for "some":

Reading the conclusion from the two lower circles, we find that there's at least one letter in Kim's name that matches a letter in Susan's name, because there's a bar in the overlap:

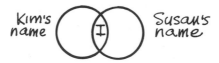

This is a possible solution:

*Names*
George Jones
Kim Johannsen
Susan Jay

(Notice that there's only one *n* in the diagrams although there are three in Kim's name and one in George's. In using the diagrams we're concerned not with how many letters there are but only with how many *different* ones and which ones match.)

In this solution, Kim's name and Susan's have, in fact, two letters in common, the *j* and the *a*. Without knowing what their names were, you could not tell this from the Venn diagrams. The only thing you could be sure of was that there was at least one letter in the segment where the *j* appears; there might or might not be any in the section where the *a* is.

Can a conclusion always be found from information of this kind? Try this one:

No letters in George's name are in Harry's name.
No letters in Harry's name are in Sarah's name.

Harry's name has the middle circle this time, because it appears in both sentences. Since his name and George's have no letters in common, shade the overlapping section of the two circles to show that that section is empty:

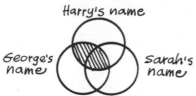

Do the same for the overlap of Harry's and Sarah's circles:

Trying to read a conclusion from the two bottom circles, we find there is none, the overlap is neither empty—it's not

fully shaded—nor does it have a bar in it to show there's
something there. Either of these two kinds of solutions is
possible:

*Names*
George Jones
Harry Buck
Sarah Elder

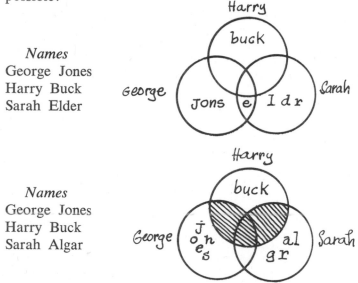

*Names*
George Jones
Harry Buck
Sarah Algar

Sarah's name and George's may or may not have letters
in common.

But lest you think that the trouble with the information
in the second case was that both statements were negative,
work this one through to a conclusion. It has one:

None of the letters in Charles' name are in Fran's.
There are no letters in George's name that are not
also in Charles'.

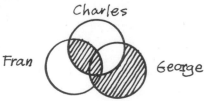

It's clear that George's name and Fran's have no letters in common. But were you really tricked? Can you restate the second sentence so that it does not contain a negative?

Here's a final group to try on the diagrams:

Some letters in Sam's name match those in Roger's.
No letters in Susan's name are not in Roger's.

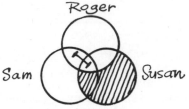

There is no conclusion, because you cannot tell from the diagrams whether the letter (or letters) that appear both in Sam's name and in Roger's also appear in Susan's. Here are two possible solutions:

*Names*
Sam Tutt
Roger Buckeram
Susan Baker

*Names*
Sam Tuttle
Roger Buckeram
Susan Baker

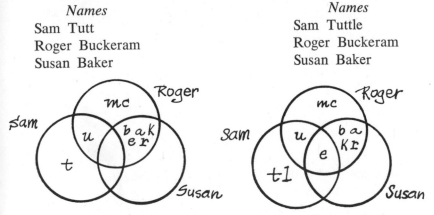

What works for discovering conclusions about whether names have letters in common works also for discovering conclusions that can be drawn from other kinds of statements. Suppose these are your agreed facts:

All worms are squirmy.
No squirmy things are delicious.

Put the squirmy things in the middle circle because they
appear in both sentences. Put the information from the
first sentence in the circles:

Then add the information from the second sentence:

To read a conclusion from the two bottom circles, copy
them leaving any section blank that is not *fully* shaded and
has no bar in it. The conclusion then looks like this:

It stands for either "No worms are delicious" or "No
delicious things are worms."

This conclusion results from an argument known as a
syllogism. The rules for syllogisms were developed by
Aristotle in the fourth century B.C. and still form the basis
for a very large part of logical argument. A syllogism

always has a conclusion which is drawn from two premises, or pieces of information. The premises may either be facts or ideas. In the diagrams we've just used, the premises were:

> All worms are squirmy.
> No squirmy things are delicious.

According to the rules of Aristotle, there are only four basic ways of stating a premise, and the same four basic ways of stating a conclusion. These four are listed below and are labeled with the first four vowels, *A, E, I* and *O*. They are called the *A, E, I* and *O* propositions:

> *A*. All goffs are flogs.
> *E*. No goffs are flogs.
> *I*. Some goffs are flogs.
> *O*. Some goffs are not flogs.

The *A* and *E* propositions do not say anything about the existence of goffs or flogs. They simply say that if there are any goffs, they are flogs (*A*) or they're not (*E*). The *I* and *O* propositions do say that there is at least one goff and that it is also a flog (*I*) or that there's one that's not a flog (*O*). From the *I* and *O* propositions we know that goffs exist but we are told only about some of them. The others may be alike or different.

This is how the four propositions look on Venn diagrams:

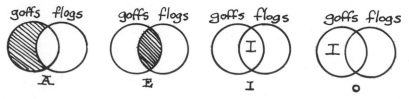

(Of course the *I* diagram can be read "some flogs are goffs" but it is customary to put the subject of the sentence in the left hand circle and read from left to right as one usually does.)

If the argument is valid—logically correct—each of your premises will look like one of these diagrams and so will your conclusion. If your conclusion, which is read from the two bottom circles, doesn't look like any of these four, it is an invalid conclusion. (By the way, an in-*val*-id conclusion is one that's not valid. You might say it had a broken leg but it's not bedridden, so don't call it *in*-val-id.)

VALID          IN-**VAL'**-ID          **IN'**-VAL-ID

In looking at the two lower circles of any diagram to find if there is a valid conclusion, remember that if a section isn't fully shaded, it's not empty.

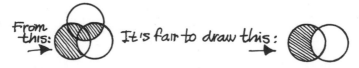

From this: ➝ *It's fair to draw this:* ➝

If there's a bar anywhere in a section, the section is occupied, but if a bar straddles two sections, you have no useful information.

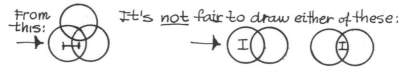

From this: ➝ *It's not fair to draw either of these:* ➝

Taking a pair of premises that resemble the last pair we used, we come up with no conclusion:

> All worms are squirmy.
> No worms are delicious.

It looks as though we should be able to conclude that no delicious things are squirmy. To do so, we'd have to end with the two lower circles looking like this:

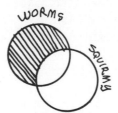

But let's see what *does* happen. Worms are the middle term. The first premise looks like this:

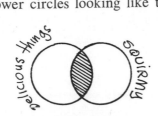

Adding the second premise gives us this:

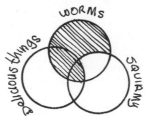

There is no conclusion. And it's reasonable (as well as logical) because nothing in the premises gave any clue as to whether eels are delicious.

In practicing with the diagrams to learn to recognize a valid argument, it is better to deal with syllogisms whose conclusions are not obviously true. If you know in advance that the conclusion is true, you may be led to believe that the argument is valid. It may not be. It's quite possible to have true premises, a true conclusion and a thoroughly invalid argument. Here's a far-out example:

$2 \times 3 = 6$
Albany is the capital of New York.
Therefore: Milk comes from cows.

On the other hand, if you believe a conclusion to be false, you may try to find fault with the argument instead of recognizing that the argument is valid but the premises are false. Here's one that might fool you:

All creatures with fur have four legs.
No creatures with four legs have wings.
Therefore: No creatures with fur have wings.

It's a valid argument. Here's how it checks out on the diagrams:

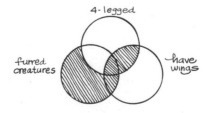

But what about bats?

So that you will not judge the validity of arguments according to your acceptance of the conclusion, here are some wacky arguments to test out on the diagrams. Are the proposed conclusions correct; that is, do they follow necessarily from the premises? Match your bottom circles against the goff-flog propositions to see if they do.

1.  Premises: No intelligent dogs eat spiders.
    All my dogs are intelligent.
    Proposed conclusion: None of my dogs eat spiders.
2.  Premises: All long-haired males are peace-loving.
    Some cats are long-haired males.
    Proposed conclusion: Some peace-lovers are cats.
3.  Premises: No hard-shelled creatures are sympathetic.
    Some crabs are hard-shelled.
    Proposed conclusion: Some crabs are unsympathetic.
4.  Premises: All chocolate-covered food makes me sick.
    Some grasshoppers do not make me sick.
    Proposed conclusion: Some grasshoppers are not chocolate-covered.
5.  Premises: All fish enjoy gumdrops.
    Some fish are ferocious.
    Proposed conclusion: Some ferocious creatures enjoy gumdrops.

To check your answers, see the end of the chapter. These, you will remember, are the diagrams your two lower circles have to match so that your conclusion can be in proper form as an *A, E, I* or *O* proposition:

A          E          I          o

Just as in the case of the name-matching, there are some pairs of premises that will yield a conclusion and some that won't. From which of the following pairs of premises can a conclusion be drawn? If you can draw one, can you state what it is?

6. Premises: All elected officials are politicians.
   Some statesmen are not elected officials.

7. Premises: All pets are tame animals.
   Some raccoons are tame animals.

8. Premises: All pets are tame animals.
   Some raccoons are pets.

9. Premises: All drug addicts need a lot of money for drugs.
   Some people who need money will steal to get it.

10. Premises: Some users of SMILE toothpaste are beautiful.
    My whole family uses SMILE toothpaste.

11. Premises: All good chisels have sharp edges.
    No chisels used as levers have sharp edges.

12. Premises: No persons under sixteen can drive a car.
    Some high school students are over sixteen.

13. Premises: No true conclusion can be drawn from false premises.
    Both of these premises are false.

The answers are at the end of the chapter, but don't look till you've done them all. If you've got more than three conclusions, try again. And if the last one gave you trouble, you're on your way to becoming a good logician. You'll find its problem dealt with in the next chapter. Dealt with, yes. For better or for worse? Turn a few pages and see.

## ANSWERS

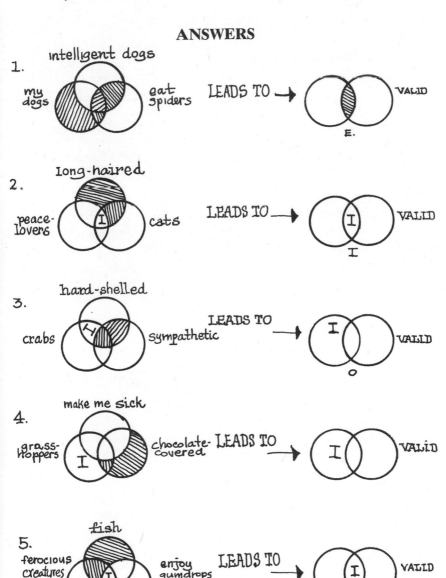

6. NO CONCLUSION.

7. NO CONCLUSION.

8. Some Raccoons
   are Tame Animals.

9. NO CONCLUSION.

10. NO CONCLUSION,

11. Good Chisels are
    not used as Levers.

12. NO CONCLUSION.

13. No True Conclusion
    can be drawn from
    these Premises.

# 3

# *You Can't Get There from Here*

There are three outlandish animals of the logical world:
the fallacy, the paradox and the dilemma. If you were to
try to draw pictures of these imaginary animals, the fallacy
would turn out to be a creature whose head was where his
tail ought to be, and there would be a lot of unexplained
bumps and protrusions on his body. He might have some
extra eyebrows, perhaps over his mouth, and a number of
useless and ungainly appendages. Any error in logic can be
called a fallacy. You have already encountered some of
them. More will appear in later chapters, since they are a
very numerous species, with many breeds. Since there are
so many, you can draw a fallacy in just about any way you
want to, as long as something is missing or misplaced.

This chapter will deal with the two rarer creatures in
the logical zoo. (Is *that* why they call it a *zoological* gar-
den?) A paradox is rather like a cassowary. Have you ever
seen a cassowary at the zoo? It's a bird, something like
an ostrich, but with a blue-orange-green-purple neck. The
more you look at it, the more you don't believe it. That's
how it is with the paradox: It can't possibly be true, but it
can't be false either. And since every statement has to be
one or the other, where are you?

the fallacy          the paradox          the dilemma

For example: "I always lie and I'm lying now," says the weird bird. If the weird bird's statement is taken as true, then he *is* lying (that's the truth he told) and so the statement has to be false (because he lied). If the weird bird's statement is taken as false, then it's not true that he's lying now, so he must be telling the truth, and therefore he *is* lying. And if you turn around three times and look again, the cassowary is *still* there with its blue-orange-green-purple neck.

You'll find dilemmas housed in nearby *zoological* cages, because the species are distantly related. Ever since the time of the Greek logicians, people have been caught on the horns of a dilemma, so we know at least that much about how our imaginary creature should be pictured. It has two horns and there is a considerable space between them. We know this because, right down from the Greek tradition, there are only two ways to escape from a dilemma: Grab both horns at once or slip between them. While there are several kinds of dilemmas, the most well known are situations that present just two choices, and both choices are unfavorable. It's a game of coin-tossing in which the rules are: Heads he wins; tails I lose.

A common sort of dilemma is one your friend Bob faced on the afternoon before a dance. He hadn't been planning to go to the dance because his family had scheduled a camping weekend. But the day dawned cold and rainy, the camping trip was postponed, and Bob wanted to go to the dance but he didn't have a date. He reasoned this way: "It's no good trying to get a date at this late hour. If a girl is attractive and pleasant, she's already got a date. If she's still free at this hour, I wouldn't want a date with her. But I don't want to go to the dance alone. . . ."

Dealing with paradoxes and dilemmas is a little like walking the edge of a Moebius strip—the longer you travel on the outside rim the further inside you find yourself, until, of course, you get outside again and then the further you go, the more you're inside.*

"You can't get there from here," is what the Vermont farmer is supposed to have told the tourist who was asking for directions. But the sentence really belongs to Zeno of Elea, the Greek philosopher of the fifth century B.C., who

* *Note*: If you've never come across a Moebius strip, please be introduced: Cut a strip of paper about an inch wide and ten inches long. *Any* size will do, but this is convenient. Make one twist in this strip and then fasten the ends together with tape so that the join lies flat. Starting at the tape, on the outside of this twisted ring, measure a third of the way across the width of the ring and draw a line parallel to the long

edge all the way back to the tape. Where are you now? Change to a different colored pencil and continue to draw the line till you get back to the tape again. It has nothing to do with logic but, if you've stayed with it this far, please take a pair of scissors and cut all the way around on the lines you've drawn and see what happens. At the risk of losing you permanently, we suggest that you now cut the thicker section lengthwise into equal strips.

said, in effect, "You can't get anywhere from here." Suppose you would just like to walk across the room and get to the opposite wall. Not possible. Obviously, before you can get all the way across, you have to get half way across. But even if you could do that—quite impossible—you would then have to cover half the remaining distance. But even if you could do that, you would then have to cover half of the balance. Half of the distance always remains to be covered before you can cover the whole distance. You'll never make it. (Or not, at least, till you get to calculus, which Zeno, of course, never did.)

When Achilles, the swiftest of runners, raced the tortoise, he gave him a handicap to make the race more equal, according to Zeno. That handicap was Achilles' undoing and clinched the race in favor of the tortoise. Clearly, before Achilles can overtake the tortoise he must first reach the place where the tortoise started. But by the time he gets there, the tortoise has gone on ahead. So Achilles must reach the place where the tortoise is then. But when he gets there, the tortoise is gone again. And so forth, and so forth. Just as the last car of the train can never overtake the engine, so Achilles will never catch up with the tortoise.

These are the most famous paradoxes of Zeno. As you can see from them, the logical paradox is an argument wherein the premises seem to be acceptable and each step of the proof appears to be valid, but the conclusion is a hopeless contradiction or is pure nonsense.

Other simple statements whose meanings are well understood can be turned into paradoxes if you examine them closely:

"Monitors are in charge of this class," says the teacher, "and no one is to leave the room until I return."

"You can't go," says Alec (known to his friends as Alexander the Great, to his enemies as Smart Alec).

"And why not?" asks the teacher, who hasn't yet learned to ignore Alec.

"Because you're not back yet, and you said no one could leave until you return."

If students are absent when the teacher goes over the math homework for correction in class, Alec is asked to correct their homework for them. Simply stated, it is Alec's job to correct the math homework of anyone who does not correct his own homework. Whose job is it to correct Alec's homework? It can't be Alec's, because he corrects the homework of those who *don't* correct their own. It can't be anyone else's job, because it's *his* job, since Alec's the only one who corrects the homework of others.

The best known of modern paradoxes is that invented by the philosopher Bertrand Russell. In simplified form, his paradox runs this way:

Basically, there are two kinds of sets. There is the ordinary set, like the set of all cats, which does not contain itself as a member. (A set of cats isn't itself a cat.) Then there are some special sets which do contain themselves as members. For instance, the set of all sets obviously does. It is a set and all sets are members of the set of all sets. The set of all phrases in the English language is a special set. It contains itself as a member since "the set of all phrases in the English language" is a phrase in the English language.

One could start a list of all possible sets and place each into one of the two columns, ordinary or special:

|  *Ordinary sets* | *Special sets* |
|---|---|
| {cat} | {all English phrases} |

From these two columns, once you had filled in a reasonable amount, you could construct two super-sets: Set *O,* the set of all ordinary sets, and set $S$, the set of all special sets.

Set $O$ = { set of cats, set of capitals of states, set of counting numbers, etc. }

Set $S$ = { set of all English phrases, set of all sets, set of all words you have ever read, etc. }

Now the question is: Does the set of all ordinary sets, Set $O$, belong in Set $O$ or Set $S$? It must go into one or the other because all sets are either ordinary or special. It can't go into Set $O$ because Set $O$ contains as members only those sets that do *not* include themselves as members and if you put Set $O$ into Set $O$ it will include itself, and the rule will be broken. On the other hand, it can't go into Set $S$, because Set $S$ contains only those sets which have themselves as members. If Set $O$ has itself as a member, then of course Set $O$ is in Set $O$, not in Set $S$, and it can't be in both. But it's not in Set $O$ because Set $O$ contains only those sets which don't have themselves as members. . . . The merry-go-round is still turning. Do you want to go around again?

What leads to paradoxes of this kind is the careless use of terms like "all," "none," "every." "Never say never" and "Every rule has exceptions" are familiar examples. When you say "Nobody understands me" do you mean "nobody" or "nobody but me"? What conclusion *can* be drawn from the final set of premises given in the last chapter?

Outside the framework of the boxed-in thinking of the syllogism, beware of accepting premises about "all" or "none" of anything. You'll find that that innocent-looking paradox bird has teeth, and if it grabs you, it will whirl you around till you're dizzy.

A dilemma will paralyze you.

While a paradox will make you dizzy, a dilemma will paralyze you. When all the choices of action you are given are either impossible or unwelcome, it's likely you'll do nothing at all. Will you turn on the light to see better how animals behave in the dark? If you want to know exactly how much air pressure there is in a tire, you have to insert a gauge. But inserting a gauge lets out some of the air. To measure a very tiny object, you need a micrometer. But the very act of measuring the object with the micrometer may change its measurement if the jaws of the micrometer compress it. These are true situational dilemmas and they cannot be solved by argument. If they are to be solved, it will be by attacking the problem head on and inventing a new way of doing things. To escape between the horns of the dilemma is to find a third alternative so that you can reject both of the choices offered and still get something done. To see how animals behave in the dark, for example, the Bronx Zoo illuminates them with red light; people can see by this light but the animals react to the light as they do to darkness.

Other dilemmas are figments that can be shooed away by refusing to accept the premises in the form in which they're offered. How would you shoo away the following dilemma?

If you know how to spell a word, you don't need to look it up in the dictionary. If you don't know how to spell it, you won't be able to find it in the dictionary. So, either way, a dictionary is not useful to anyone for finding out how to spell a word.

Just as some people get along well with cats and aren't specially fond of dogs, while others always seem to attract dogs and to be attracted to them, so certain people are partial to dilemmas and dilemmas tend to follow them home. Other people can walk away from dilemmas without a backward glance. Which type are you? Suppose you want a bike and are reading the "for sale" ads in the local paper to see if you could pick up a second-hand one. It's ten in the morning and it's last night's paper you're reading. How do you respond to the following ad:

> English bike. Good condition. $15.
> Call mornings. 999-1111.

Do you pick up the phone? If you're a dilemma-lover, you'll reason this way: If the bike was any good someone will have bought it already, so there's no point in calling. If the advertiser still has it for sale, it's not worth the money, so why bother?

A student who is a dilemma-lover often runs into situations like this: The teacher has given him a note to take home, describing his misbehavior in school. If he gives the note to his parents, he will be punished for the misbehavior. If he doesn't give them the note, sooner or later they'll find out and he'll be punished for not giving it to them.

Alec would solve this one by answering a dilemma with a dilemma. The conversation between Alec and his Dad might go like this:

"Laws and rules of conduct are very baffling to me, Dad."

"Oh? In what way?"

"Well, sometimes you get punished for doing something and sometimes for not doing something. It doesn't make sense."

"What are you talking about? When do you get punished for not doing something?"

"Lots of times, Dad. Like not getting a fishing license or not paying your income tax."

"Well, yes. But what's so puzzling about that? If you're supposed to do something and you don't do it, why shouldn't you be punished?"

"But, Dad, what about the situations where you get punished for doing or not doing the very same thing. If you do it, you're punished and if you don't do it you're punished."

"There aren't any situations like that. That's ridiculous."

"Are you sure?"

"Of course I'm sure. If it's a crime, don't do it, but if it's the right thing to do, do it. Nobody's going to punish you for failing to commit a crime and nobody's going to punish you for doing the right thing."

"Guaranteed?"

"Guaranteed."

"O.K. I accept your guarantee. The right thing to do is to give you this note from my teacher, and you've just guaranteed that I can't be punished as a result. Thanks, Dad. I've always known you were fair."

If Alec had happened to encounter his mother before his father got home, the conversation might have gone this way:

"Mother, if I guess correctly what you're going to do next, will you promise not to punish me?"

"Well of course, Alec, why should I punish you?"

"I don't know, but will you promise?"

"I promise, silly boy. Now let's see you guess what I'm going to do next."

"My teacher told me to give you this note as soon as I got home, and my guess is that you're going to read it."

As you can see, Alec has had considerable experience with dilemmas and is a past master in the art of handling them. For him dilemmas practically sit up and beg, and when he's in serious trouble he just whistles for one. Once he was in bad trouble. He'd been accused of some dreadful deed and his teacher was sputtering with fury.

"I've had just about enough of you, Alec, you and your lying, sneaking ways. This time you've gone too far. I'll give you just one chance to say something and it had better be the truth. If you tell me the truth, I'll only keep you after school as punishment. But if you lie to me in this one chance I'm giving you, I'll see to it that you're suspended for five days beginning right this minute. Are you going to be a man and tell the truth or are you going to try to lie your way out? Speak up! You've got one chance."

How did Alec avoid both punishments?

For Alec, it was simple. He had a chance to say just one thing. He said it. "You will suspend me," he said.

If the statement Alec made was true, then he could not be suspended, because he was given the chance to make just one statement and was promised that if he spoke the truth, his punishment would be detention, not suspension. But if what he said was a lie—meriting suspension—then "You will suspend me" was a lie, so he wasn't suspended. He couldn't be kept after school for the lie, either, because detention was the punishment if he told the truth.

The end of this particular story is shrouded in mystery because it is not known whether Alec's teacher managed to keep his devotion to formal logic even when he was in a sputtering rage. Few teachers do.

# 4

# *All Right-Thinking People Believe*

"If you talk to me while I'm adding these figures, I'll get the wrong answer, so keep quiet." After a period of silence: "O.K. Done now. Thank goodness you didn't talk to me. Now I know my answer's right."

If you want to name this kind of fallacy—or error in logical proof—you might call it the fallacy of the single cause. Is there really no other possible reason why the answer might be wrong? Reversing the argument gives a result that's just as phony: "I got the wrong answer. It must be because you talked to me while I was adding."

Circumstantial evidence is often like this. A murder has been committed. A button was found at the scene of the crime. If the button came off the coat of the accused, it will match the remaining buttons on his coat. It *does* match them, therefore the accused must be guilty. In a later chapter you will find the directions for making a computer to check out errors of this kind, just as earlier examples of fallacies could be checked out on the Venn diagrams.

But not all fallacies are caused by errors in logical proof. Some, for example, depend on the peculiarities of language and grammar. What's wrong with this syllogism? In logical form it's faultless:

Words of five letters are bigger than words of four
letters.
Seven is a word of five letters and nine is a word of
four letters.
Therefore: Seven is bigger than nine.

Sometimes words change meaning in the course of the
argument in ways not quite so obvious:

No two-year-olds are as tall as high school students.
Some race horses are two-year-olds.
Therefore: Some race horses are not as tall as high
school students.

The trouble here is that the premises have not been written out in full. If they had been, you could see that there
are four terms, one too many: two-year-old humans, high
school students, race horses, and two-year-old horses.

The word "is" often causes confusion. Sentences in
exactly the same form express very different relationships.
"Brazil is the largest country in South America" reverses
readily to "The largest country in South America is Brazil."
But the sentence "A dog is an animal" does not reverse to
"An animal is a dog." Does "is" mean "equivalent to" or
"is included in the class of"?

If John is a brother of George and George is a brother of
Sam, then John is a brother of Sam. Does it follow that if

John is a friend of George and George is a friend of Sam, that John is a friend of Sam?

Just because something is true of a class or group of people, does it necessarily follow that it's true of every member of the group?

> The citizens of New York are of many different national backgrounds.
> Joe Doakes is a citizen of New York.
> Therefore: Joe Doakes is of many different national backgrounds.

Try another:

> Accidents are frequent occurrences.
> The explosion of a fuel tank on an Apollo mission was an accident.
> Therefore: The explosion of a fuel tank on an Apollo mission is a frequent occurrence.

And one more:

> Temperatures on July days are higher than on days in May.
> On May 24, the temperature was 95°.
> Therefore: I predict that July days this year will have temperatures of over 95°.

Some logical fallacies are just the result of sloppy thinking. A little practice with the diagrams will give you the ammunition to shatter the sloppy thinker's argument. But other fallacies are deliberately used as tricks to win arguments. To hold your own against the skilled user of logical fallacies, you must first learn to spot the fallacy, to catch the word-magician in the act of putting into the hat the rabbit he's later going to pull out of it.

When he has no premise to support his conclusion, the tricky arguer just assumes his conclusion to be true and hopes you won't notice: "My reason for saying that Brand X is popular is that so many people like it."

"Have you stopped beating your wife?" is the hoariest example of "begging the question" as this fallacy of circular reasoning is called. Can the trickster extract some money from an acquaintance who has borrowed nothing from him by saying very sternly, "When are you going to pay me back what you owe me?"

Someone who has no facts to support his proposed conclusion that Frenchmen are more romantic than Germans might say, "Why do you suppose Frenchmen are so much more romantic than Germans?" hoping to lead you into a discussion of possible causes and thus to avoid having to prove that they are.

When you don't fall for this trick of circular argument, the sneaky logician may try to get you on his side with an *ad hominem* argument. If he has no good reasons with which to persuade you to accept his conclusion, he will address himself *to the man* (*ad hominem* is the Latin translation) rather than to the argument. He wants you to vote for the town's purchase of the Wetmarsh property for the new school but you've been listening to some good arguments against it. "Oh," he says, "so Mr. Childless opposes the building of a new school on the Wetmarsh property? What does it matter what his reasons are? He has no children in school so of course he's against it."

Sometimes the *ad hominem* argument attacks the supporters of the argument: "You eat corn? Why so do pigs!" Sometimes it attempts to flatter you into accepting a conclusion: "A discriminating person like you wouldn't dream of settling for less than the best, so if you can't afford this luxury, buy now, pay later." "You're a union man and have always sided with the working people, so I know you won't vote for the playground when you know that the sponsors of that program are all presidents of corporations."

Close to the *ad hominem* fallacy is the appeal to authority: All right thinking people believe this so of course you do too. More doctors recommend. . . . All the best people buy. . . . This is the floor wax most often used by Hollywood stars. . . . The President supports this candidate. . . .

"Because I say so" may be a suitable answer for a father to give to his five-year-old son, but it is not a very good argument. Does it become any better when it is revised to read, "Because Mr. Big says so"?

Watch out for arguments that cannot stand on their own feet. What sort of props are used to hold them up? When a speaker says, "This fact is so well known that it needs no proof," you may interpret his statement to mean that he *has* no proof.

The trickster who can't answer the question with evidence and logic very cleverly avoids the question entirely. An evening with TV commercials can provide an excellent short course in spotting logical fallacies of this kind. What sort of reasons are given for preferring one product over another? Watch the pretty child grow before your eyes from age two to age twelve as she eats the product that builds strong bodies twelve ways. (Name *one* way?) Why does the attractive model use this hairspray? Because it makes her feel more like herself. Why is this toothpaste better than others? It contains a secret ingredient—and no one will tell you the secret.

A more subtle way of avoiding the question is by changing the subject and hoping that the change won't be noticed: The high school football field needs a new drainage system because it's unusable for three days after every heavy rain. "What! Spend $1800 on a drainage system! Do you realize that people are starving in India?"

An appeal to emotion, all by itself, is not a logical fallacy, any more than a toy gun is a dangerous weapon. But when the toy gun is used in a holdup, when it *pretends* to be a real gun, it becomes a dangerous weapon. Just so, an appeal to emotion which pretends to be a logical argument is a fallacy. Appeals to emotion are fine in their place. Of course you're more likely to contribute time and money to a campaign to save the baby seals, or to make possible research to prevent disease, or to provide fresh-air camps for city children if your sympathy or pity is aroused by a picture of those you're asked to help. An appeal to emotion undoubtedly works better than logic to prove you ought to help, but logic is far more useful in finding out how best to give help. Will the picture answer that question?

Appeals to prejudice are as effective as appeals to emotion. What are the reasons for and against an all-volunteer army? Is it helpful in resolving the question to say either, "Don't trust anyone over thirty," or "Why bother to listen to anyone who doesn't even take the trouble to put on a proper shirt and tie?" It may not be *logically* helpful, but votes for or against an issue are often gained by such "arguments."

Just as the magician depends on his ability to keep your attention focused on something showy and irrelevant while he is quietly doing some simple thing to effect his trick, so the tricky arguer is trying to divert your attention by appealing to your emotions and prejudices. He should not be able to fool you if you take the time to check out the steps in his reasoning. On the other hand there's another group of fallacies whose reasoning, in a formal sense, is faultless, but. . . .

In the folklore of every country there are stories of wise men who come up with strange solutions to problems. The wise men of Gotham, for example, were always wary of leaving their homes for long trips through the English countryside, fearing that someone would break the lock on the door and steal their possessions while they were away. One of the wise men had a solution. He removed his front door from its hinges and carried it with him, lock and all. That way, no one could break the lock.

The wise man was perfectly logical, but nobody's likely to take his advice seriously. But where, exactly, is the point where nonsense begins? Take it seriously for a moment and set it up this way:

| *Problem* | *Solution* |
|---|---|
| How shall I prevent a burglar from breaking the lock on my front door while I'm away? | Remove the front door with its lock and take it with me so no burglar can get to it. |

The following situations and their solutions follow the same pattern of problem and solution. Are any of them ridiculous? All of them?

|     *Problem*     |     *Solution*     |
|---|---|

1. There has been a bottleneck in the office. Letters that were typed up last week have still not been mailed out. Customers complain that they receive letters dated ten days earlier than the date of arrival.

Don't date the letters when you type them. Use a date stamp when you mail them.

2. The session of the State Assembly is due to end at midnight, but many important proposed laws have not yet been voted on.

Set the clock back a few hours so there will be time to vote on important bills before the hands of the clock reach twelve.

3. Helen doesn't understand the work in algebra. She has failed three tests in a row and she will probably fail the course.

On the next test day, sit next to Sue, an honor student, and copy her answers.

4. There must be something wrong with the electric iron because every time Mother plugs it in, the fuse blows. We've used up three fuses already.

Put a penny underneath the next fuse. It won't burn out so easily.

5. I can't bear to look at how those poor people in the ghetto live —not enough to eat, no proper clothes, rats all over the uncollected garbage.

Build a high wall between your neighborhood and theirs, and then you won't be able to see it.

All of these, as you surely have guessed, are actually solutions people have used to solve their problems. They are not folk tales. What is wrong with the logic?

Suppose someone comes into your house and says, "I think I smell gas. Are you sure you don't have an open unlit burner on the stove? The smell of gas is quite strong." Would you answer, "Oh, you smell gas! How dreadful! I wouldn't want my house to smell bad; I'll open a bottle of air freshener"?

Or suppose you went to a doctor and said, "Look at this raw, red gash I have across my face. I cut and bruised myself running into a wire fence." Would you be satisfied if the doctor said, "Oh, yes, it is rather red and ugly, isn't it? I have several shades of flesh-colored face cream. Let's test them out and see which shade most nearly matches your skin tones. We'll paint it on and the gash will be almost invisible."

All of these situations are examples of sweeping the dirt under the rug instead of cleaning it out. A doctor would say they are examples of treating the symptom rather than the disease. If the disease cannot be treated because no cure has yet been found, as in the case of the common cold, it may be helpful to treat the symptom. Then, at least, the patient feels better, temporarily. But a cold, whether treated or not, will usually cure itself in a couple of weeks. Where the disease is more serious and persistent and where a cure can be found, to treat only the symptom makes little more sense than to carry your front door with you on your travels.

When a person solves his problem by treating the symptom rather than the disease it is usually because he doesn't understand what his problem is. He sees only the surface difficulty, not its cause. There are other situations involving fallacies of logical reasoning in which the problem *is* understood but there is no comprehension of how to go about curing the disease. Mr. Reasoner's life is full of examples.

Here is Mr. Reasoner driving along the highway at fifty miles per hour. He looks down at the gas gauge and sees that it reads "Empty." "Oh, no!" he says to himself, "I know this road. It's ten miles to the nearest gas station. At the rate I'm going it'll take me about twelve minutes to get there and the gas I have in my tank will never last twelve minutes." So he steps on the gas and goes seventy-five miles per hour to try to get to the gas station before he runs out of gas. It won't work, as you know, because the faster he goes, the more gas he will use.

When Mr. Reasoner paints his house, he puts on two coats of paint, one right after the other as he goes along, so as to save time and not have to keep moving the ladder back and forth. Mr. and Mrs. Reasoner are a happy couple because they think alike. Mrs. Reasoner often tries to cook a roast in half the time by setting the oven at twice the recommended temperature. She drives ten miles to buy a can of soup because it's two cents cheaper in that store than in her local grocery.

Mrs. Reasoner devotes one evening a week to volunteer work in the hospital, and she is the nurse's aid who wakes the patient up to give him a sleeping pill.

The Reasoners were expecting weekend guests and had been busy all morning with their chores. The sky was overcast and it looked as if it might start to rain at any moment. Mr. Reasoner, well aware that outdoor chores are not pleasant to do in the rain, was hurrying to get his gardening done and made every effort to set up the sprinkler system before the rain came down. Meanwhile Mrs. Reasoner was indoors waiting impatiently for the phone to ring to announce that the guests had arrived at the bus station and were waiting for the Reasoners to pick them up. She got very bored and fidgety with the waiting so she decided to while the time away by phoning a few friends.

Mr. and Mrs. Reasoner are great believers in democracy and firmly believe in the representative form of government. When they go to the voting booth, they both vote for a dull-witted candidate for senator, since they want their senator to be representative of them. And when their candidate is elected, as he often is, he is among those who vote to confirm the nomination of a mediocre judge to the Supreme Court, saying, in support of the motion to confirm, "There are a lot of mediocre judges and people and lawyers, and they are entitled to a little representation, aren't they? We can't have all Brandeises and Frankfurters and Cardozos."

The Reasoners agree with their senator. They also assume that the Superintendent of Schools will look for a retarded person to teach the class of retarded children.

And, of course, they're certain that a Communist's lawyer is himself a Communist. "After all," Mr. Reasoner pointed out, "Birds of a feather flock together."

The Reasoners are fond of proverbs like this. They seem to solve so many difficult situations so simply. And, since proverbs have come down from generation to generation and have stood the test of time, they must be true and reliable guides to conduct.

Once or twice, though, they have come near to quarreling. They were concerned over whether they should send their son to camp for the summer. Perhaps he would become so involved with strangers that he would forget them and love them less. "Don't worry," Mr. Reasoner said. "Absence makes the heart grow fonder." But Mrs. Reasoner argued that her mother had always quoted, "Out of sight, out of mind."

Once, when they were offered a chance to invest all their savings in the stock of a new and promising company at a special in-on-the-ground-floor price, they spent a very troubled evening. "Opportunity knocks but once." "Look before you leap." "He who hesitates is lost." "Don't put all your eggs in one basket." "Nothing ventured, nothing gained." *Which* was right for the occasion?

Mr. & Mrs. Reasoner

# 5

# *Knock It Down, Build It Up*

❄

Faced with a new gadget whose workings you don't fully understand, it's often easier to begin by tearing it down to find out what makes it go. Once you've torn it down and put the pieces into proper piles, you can figure out how to build it up again. That way, the instructions for assembling the gadget might even make sense.

The first step in tearing an argument down is to get the premises into shape for placement in the circles or the boxes. In ordinary conversation people seldom speak in sentences that take precisely the form of the *A, E, I* and *O* propositions, but many of the things they say can be readily translated into these forms. Then the validity of the argument can be tested. Here's a bit of catty conversation that can be checked out:

"Do you know whether Helen has a prom date?"

"Well, I don't *know,* but I doubt it. All of the attractive girls have prom dates, but nobody would call Helen attractive."

Bring out the Venn diagrams. There seem to be three categories: attractive girls, Helen, and those who have prom dates. Since the proposed conclusion is "Helen doesn't have a prom date," "attractive girls" must be the middle term that is to disappear. How does it look?

Helen may or may not have a prom date, but this argument certainly doesn't resolve the question. The premises lead to no conclusion.

"What on earth is a frazzleberry frostwhip?"

"Oh, it's gooey and I love it, but, like all the things I adore, it makes John sick."

"Hey, Bob! You should have one. Whatever John can't stand is just your bag."

You can tune in tomorrow to find out if Bob likes frazzleberry frostwhip, or you can check it out now. There's an even stronger conclusion to be discovered:

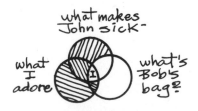

The *I* is there because frazzleberry frostwhip is definitely one thing I adore that makes John sick. Yes, Bob should have a frazzleberry frostwhip, and anything else I care to recommend because everything I adore is just Bob's bag.

"Anyone can vote unless he's under eighteen." How would you set this premise up? There are two choices:

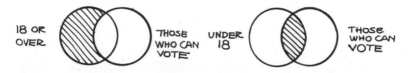

This flexibility in rewording premises is needed because sometimes an argument seems to have more categories than can be fitted into the three circles of the Venn diagrams.

Suppose you are faced with one of the conclusions in the introduction to this book and you want to argue the point. "Student protesters who disrupt the school program should be expelled!" shouts Mr. Sayso in impassioned tones.

"On what do you base your conclusion?"

"Nobody should be in school unless he's prepared to benefit from the school program," says Mr. Sayso, "and students who disrupt the program are not prepared to benefit from it. That's why!"

If you disagree with the conclusion, is it the premises of the argument you should challenge? Try the argument first because it's always more impressive to say, if you can, "Even if everything you say is true, your conclusion isn't logical." Check the argument on the diagrams. What categories will you have for the three circles? At first sight, you seem to need five:

1. people who should be in school
2. people prepared to benefit from the program
3. students who disrupt the program
4. people not prepared to benefit from the program
5. people who should be expelled

Using the boxes, it would be easy to fit in these five groups

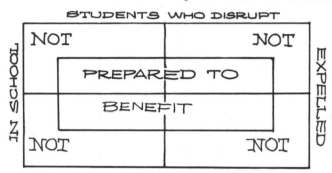

with all outside the inner box for those not prepared to benefit. For the circles, it's necessary to recognize that just as 2 and 4 are opposites, so are 1 and 5. Within the universe of discourse, which the Venn diagrams do not fence in, everything outside a circle is the opposite of what's inside it. It's easier to label the circles for people who *are* or *do* something, leaving the space outside for those who are not or do not. With this in mind, the circles can be used for

> people who should be in school (label: in school)
> students who disrupt (label: disrupters)
> people prepared to benefit from the program (label: benefiters)

Since the conclusion, as translated, is "Students who disrupt are not people who should be in school," these two categories should be placed in the two lower circles. Here is the way the argument looks on the diagrams:

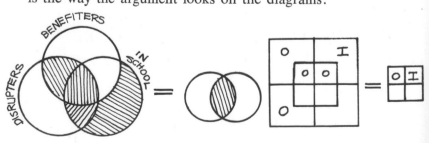

The argument is valid. If you want to disagree with the conclusion "Students who disrupt the school program should be expelled," it is the premises that you must attack. Or, if you cannot attack the premises, you might counter with this argument:

"Of course student protesters are not prepared to benefit from the school program. The school program is so hopelessly outmoded that no one can benefit from it. So, if your answer is expulsion, expel everyone."

This is a two-part argument for which you'll need two sets of diagrams.

1.
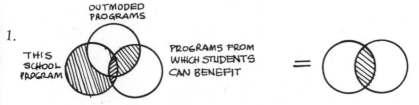

All of this school program is outmoded.
Outmoded programs are not programs that can benefit students.
Therefore this school program is a program from which no students can benefit.

2.
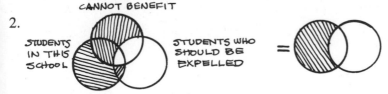

Students who cannot benefit from the school program should be expelled.

No students in this school can benefit from the program.
Therefore all students in this school should be expelled.

As the arguments on both sides become more impassioned, logic is frequently abandoned, and the larger the windbag, the more readily it can be punctured. Can you find the flaws in these samples of oratory by checking them out on the diagrams?

"Expel student protesters? That's ridiculous! Our country was founded by people who protested, and we have always honored the founders of our country. Students who protest should not be expelled; they should be honored."

Suggested form of premises:

1. Some founders of our country were protesters.
   All founders of our country are honored.
   Conclusion?
2. Use the conclusion of 1 for the first premise.
   Add: Some students are protesters.
   Conclusion?

"Student protesters favor ending the war in Vietnam. Communists favor ending the war in Vietnam. Student protesters are nothing but a bunch of Communists!"

This last one hardly needs to be checked out. It looks just like "All cats are animals and all dogs are animals, so all cats are dogs."

Many arguments in ordinary conversation get by because a premise is not expressed. If the premise were stated it would not be accepted, so it's suppressed. The trick here is to find the hidden premise and get it out in the open where it can be attacked.

"Sue can't pitch! She's a girl!"

To arrive at the conclusion, the missing premise has to be "No girls can pitch." Do you accept it? How about the members of prize-winning girls' softball teams?

"I'm no good in math. Neither was my mother." Is mathematical ability an inherited characteristic? It has to be for the argument to be valid.

Here's a syllogism from Mother Goose. Is it valid?

> Jack Sprat could eat no fat.
> His wife could eat no lean.
> And so, betwixt the both of them
> They licked the platter clean.

Did they? Not necessarily. How much was on the platter? Did they gorge themselves and eat it all? Use the circles as plates and serve the meal this way: Jack's plate of food is on the left, Mrs. Sprat's on the right. The top circle can't be the platter because there's no way to show, in a single circle, that it contains both fat and lean. You'll have to choose one or the other. If the top circle is fat, then everything outside it is lean. The information fits more easily into the boxes. Let Jack have the top half. Then the bottom half's not Jack's. Mrs. Sprat can have the left hand side and none of the right is hers. Everything in the inner square is fat and everything in the area around it is lean. The entire box, then, the universe of discourse, is the platter.

This is the information we have:

We're not told that anybody actually ate anything, but even if we assume that both did eat *something,* it doesn't really help. You can put an *I* in the top right for Jack. (The top left's already marked empty so it can't go there.) Put an *I* in the only place you can for Mrs. Sprat—inside lower left—because all the other left-hand squares are already marked empty.

The only conclusion you can reach is that Jack and his wife don't eat the same things. The platter? It may have been full or empty.

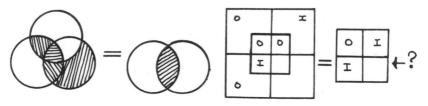

Now that you know how to knock an argument down, can you build one that will stand? How do you set up a syllogism to prove, to someone who doubts it (or to yourself), that a conclusion you've come to is true? For example, how would you prove the conclusion "Some reptiles do not lay eggs"? Always start with the conclusion and ask why. Your answer should give you the middle term.

What information do you need to support the conclusion? What reptiles are there that don't lay eggs? There are some live-bearing snakes. That will do nicely. Start with the two circles that will form your conclusion. You want it to look like this:

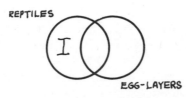

You also have the premise "Some snakes are not egg-layers." "Snakes," then, is the middle term and what is missing is a premise about snakes and reptiles. Try "Some reptiles are snakes":

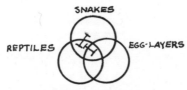

This doesn't work, because, in filling in the bar in the overlap between reptiles and snakes, there is no way of knowing whether it lies inside the egg-layer circle or it doesn't. Both premises are true, but the conclusion, also true, doesn't necessarily follow from them. Try a different true premise: "All snakes are reptiles."

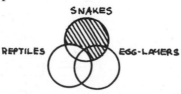

Now when you add the bar for "Some snakes do not lay eggs," there is only one remaining part of the snake circle in which you can put the bar. Putting it there does give you the conclusion you're looking for:

Let's try to build an argument to support one of the conclusions proposed in the introduction: "Smoking marijuana should not be illegal." First, translate the conclusion so it doesn't have two negatives. (You *can* diagram it the way it is but it's much easier to diagram "Smoking marijuana should be legal," and the idea is the same.) The conclusion will have to look like this:

What is needed is a middle term for premises that will scratch out sectors 3 and 6 and will leave sector 1 or 4 alone. Remember that if part of the overlap is not scratched out, the overlap is not empty and is therefore not scratched out in the conclusion.

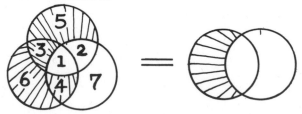

To get rid of sector 6, we must get rid of 4 *and* 6 by choosing a middle term we can use in a premise that says [all] smoking marijuana is that middle term. To get rid of sector 3, we must get rid of 3 *and* 5 by using that middle term in a premise that says all the middle term should be legal (or none of it should be illegal, which is the same thing).

Now that you have the conclusion and the form of the argument, you have to ask yourself "Why *should* smoking marijuana be legal?" If you disagree with the conclusion you probably can't find a single good reason. If you agree with it, perhaps you have many. Whether you agree or not, here's one set of premises that will fit to make the argument valid. (If the conclusion's not true, it's the premises that are at fault. If they're true, the conclusion's true. If one or both are false, the conclusion's false.)

1. The laws of a community should reflect what the majority of people in the community believe is proper conduct. Only those acts should be illegal which are disapproved by the majority.
2. The majority of people in the community believe that smoking marijuana is proper conduct.

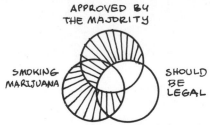

Go back to the introduction and pick some conclusions you agree with. By now you should be able to build a sturdy argument to support them.

The diagrams are useful also for checking out some arguments that do not quite fit into the syllogism form. For instance:

Everyone on the student council is either a good athlete or an *A* student, but some members of the student council are poor athletes.

It may not look that way at first, but the conclusion is there to be found: "Some *A* students are not good athletes," or "Some poor athletes are *A* students."

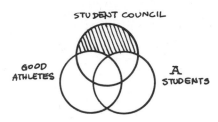

Shade in the first premise on diagram 1 to show that there are no student council members outside *both* the athlete and *A* student circles. The second premise is recorded this way:

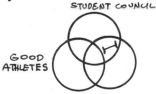

Put together, the premises look like this, and the conclusion is proved:

Sometimes you're quite certain that the information you have in your premises is sufficient to support your conclusion, but it just won't check out, though you know the conclusion is true. For example:

All copper is metal.
No copper is magnetic.
Therefore some metal is not magnetic.

The diagrams show no conclusion:

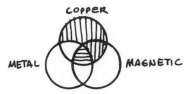

One useful trick to get around this is to reason this way: The conclusion is either true or it isn't. Let's see what happens if we assume it *isn't* true. Use the opposite of the conclusion as a new premise; use one of your premises as the second one and see what conclusion you reach in the new argument:

1. $\begin{cases}\text{All metal is magnetic} \\ \text{All copper is metal}\end{cases}$ *or* 2. $\begin{cases}\text{All metal is magnetic} \\ \text{No copper is magnetic}\end{cases}$

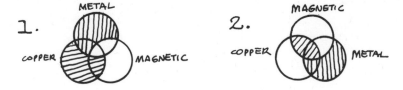

The first diagram leads to the conclusion that all copper is magnetic, a fact you know to be false because it contradicts the premise you started with. The second diagram leads to the equally false conclusion that no copper is metal. You have proved you conclusion by showing that if the opposite were true, ridiculous conclusions follow. This kind of roundabout proof is known by the Latin name *reductio ad absurdum*—reducing to the absurd or ridiculous.

All the arguments we've been using are in the form of what is called the categorical syllogism, so called because things or people are put into categories or classes. We have used such categories as "members of the student council," "creatures with fins," etc. Another form of syllogism, the conditional syllogism, goes equally well into the diagrams. Instead of saying, "All cats are mammals and all mammals are animals, therefore all cats are animals," it says, "If a cat is a mammal and if all mammals are animals, then a cat is an animal." The cat is an animal if it meets the *condition* of being a mammal, and so forth. Sometimes the argument takes this form: "If a cat is a mammal, then it is an animal." This is the same argument, but with one premise understood. It can be placed in the circles when you express the missing premise.

Take this argument: "If he wants to pass his exams, he'll study." To put this into the circles, translate it to: "All people who pass exams are people who study. He is a person who wants to pass his exams. Therefore he studies."

If a car runs, it has gas, but this car has no gas. Conclusion: This car doesn't run.

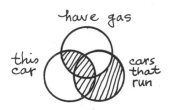

Does it work the other way? If a car runs it has gas. This car has gas. Therefore it runs.

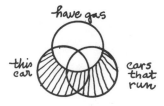

No. Not necessarily.

When arguments in the form of "If this, then that" become more complicated, they become more and more difficult to fit into the circles, and there are some kinds of arguments that will not go conveniently onto the diagrams at all. For these, a different system of checking the logic is useful. Turn the page and see.

# 6

# *Logic Turns the Floodlights On*

Until about a century ago if you were studying geometry you studied only what Euclid had taught in ancient Greece. Nothing had changed in this field of learning since about 300 B.C. And though there are new ways of studying geometry now, and new geometries to study, today's students still start with Euclid's axioms, postulates and proofs and, for the most part, the sum of the angles of a triangle is still 180°, as he said it was.

In much the same way, the principles of logic laid down by Aristotle remained, until fairly recent times, the only subject properly called logic. The boxes and the Venn diagrams we have been dealing with so far made little change in the form of the argument. Beyond allowing other verbs to be substituted for "is" and "are," they simply offered a new form in which Aristotle's principles could be stated. But when the English mathematician George Boole published *The Mathematical Analysis of Logic* in 1847 he showed the way to deal with a great variety of arguments, all the old ones and many more besides.

Some time back we pointed out that it's quite possible to have true premises and a true conclusion together making up an invalid argument. The example given was

$2 \times 3 = 6$
Albany is the capital of New York.
Therefore: Milk comes from cows.

The categorical syllogism won't let you put those three together because there is no middle term that the two premises have in common and because the conclusion doesn't contain any terms of the premises. George Boole's system will allow you to use those three statements as propositions in a single argument. It does not even matter, for the moment at least, whether any one or all of them is true or false. What is necessary is only that it is possible to have a point of view about whether each of them is true or false or to attempt to prove its truth or falsity by some reference to authority. While you can use a proposition like "clouds are the capital of oatmeal," it will not do as well because people cannot easily agree or disagree about the truth of it. Still, you could use it.

To show how the system works, let's take two statements about which we can agree that one is true and the other is false:

Pigs are animals. (We'll label it *p* for pigs)
Quadrupeds have six legs. (To be labeled *q* for quadrupeds)

What happens if the two statements are joined together? Is it true that "Pigs are animals and quadrupeds have six legs?" No, because unless each half of the joint statement is true by itself, the combination is false. But how about "Pigs are animals *or* quadrupeds have six legs"? That's true enough because the "or" gives you a choice—only one of the portions has to be true.

To write this down for use in logical exercises, symbols

are convenient. (How much math work would you get done if you had to write 23 $\times$ 476 this way: "Multiply six by three; put down the last figure of your answer; multiply seven by three and to the last figure of your answer add the first figure of your previous answer. . . ."?) Propositions in symbolic logic can be put into equations much like those in math. Only a few new symbols need to be recognized. "$\wedge$" means "and." It's easy to remember because it looks like an $A$ without the crossbar. $V$ means "or" and if there's an easy way to remember it, nobody's mentioned it. $T$ stands for true and $F$ stands for false—hardly a new idea. Propositions (whether about pigs, quadrupeds, roosters, salmon or anything else) are labeled $p, q, r, s,$ etc. What we've just put down at some length can be written this way in symbolic logic:

$p \wedge q = F$ (It is false that "pigs are animals *and* quadrupeds have six legs.")

$p \vee q = T$ (It is true that "pigs are animals *or* quadrupeds have six legs.")

One more symbol you'll need to know to get started is the squiggle that means "not": $\neg p$ means "pigs are not animals." Obviously, $\neg T = F$ and $\neg F = T$.

Here is a truth table that can be used to check the truth or falsity of combinations of any two propositions $p$ and $q$:

| p | q | p ∧ q |
|---|---|-------|
| T | T | T |
| T | F | F |
| F | T | F |
| F | F | F |

| p | q | p ∨ q |
|---|---|-------|
| T | T | T |
| T | F | T |
| F | T | T |
| F | F | F |

The first line of the left-hand table can be read this way: If $p$ is true and if $q$ is true, then $p$ *and* $q$ is true. The second line reads: If $p$ is true and if $q$ is false, then $p$ *and* $q$ is false. You will notice that only a $T$ in both columns gives a $T$ in the third column. In the second table $p$ *or* $q$ is true if either $p$ or $q$ (or both) is separately true. Only an $F$ in both the $p$ and $q$ columns produces an $F$ in the third column.

Suppose $p$ stands for "His mother is in New York" and $q$ stands *for* "Today is Friday." If today is Friday and his mother is in Newark is $p$ V $q$ true? Yes it is, according to the third row of the table. Today is Friday *or* his mother's in New York. She's not in New York, but it *is* Friday, so the proposition $p$ V $q$ is true.

To work out some logic questions it's convenient to expand the truth table to include columns for $\neg p$ and $\neg q$. The columns are easy to fill in. Since $p$ and $\neg p$ can never be both true or both false at the same time, if you fill in the columns for $p$ and $q$ first, all you have to do is fill in $F$ for $\neg p$ next to every $T$ for $p$, and $T$ for $\neg p$ next to every $F$ for $p$, etc., like this:

| $p$ | $\neg p$ | $q$ | $\sim q$ | $p$ V $\sim q$ |
|---|---|---|---|---|
| T | F | T | F | T |
| T | F | F | T | T |
| F | T | T | F | F |
| F | T | F | T | T |

Sometimes the rules of logic give meanings different from those used in ordinary conversation. If you heard someone say, "That certainly was a 1930 Ford or my name is not Harry," you would take it for granted that his name *was* Harry and that he was certain he'd just seen a 1930 Ford. Under the rules of logic, however, that needn't be the case. The sentence *could* mean what you assumed it did mean, but it could also be the case that his name was *not* Harry and the car was a 1930 Ford, or his name was *not* Harry and the car was *not* a 1930 Ford. On the truth table ($p$ V $\smallfrown$ $q$) the only way that sentence would be false would be if the speaker's name *was* Harry and the car he saw was *not* a 1930 Ford. Only row three gives *F* as the answer. All other combinations are true. But don't let it throw you. It's sensible as well as logical, because what Harry said (and who else but Harry would say it?) *is* false only if what he saw was not a 1930 Ford.

Take another form of the same kind of "I'm positive about it" statement: "That's a camel or I'm a monkey's uncle." That sentence will work out on the $p$ V $q$ table to be true only if it *was* a camel (unless the speaker *is* a monkey's uncle).

The Venn diagrams limited you to two propositions used as premises. The truth tables can be expanded indefinitely, if you have the time. Just for a little practice, on what day of the week will this sentence be true if spoken by John? If spoken by George?

"Today is Tuesday or my name is not George, or it's not Tuesday or my name is John."

$$p = \text{today is Tuesday}$$
$$q = \text{my name is George}$$
$$r = \text{my name is John}$$

On the tables, work out first $p$ V $\smallfrown$ $q$ (Today is Tuesday or my name is not George), then $\smallfrown$ $p$ V $r$ (It's not Tuesday or my name is John). If you set up the $p$ V $\smallfrown$ $q$ and the $\smallfrown$ $p$ V $r$ columns next to each other and leave a space between them, it's easy to fill that space (labeled just V) with the answers to the whole statement: ($p$ V $\smallfrown$ $q$) V ($\smallfrown$ $p$ V $r$). The rules for filling that column are the same as for any V column: Two *F*s yield an *F*; any other combination yields *T*.

| p | ~p | q | ~q | p V ~q | V | ~p V r | ~r | r | ~p | p |
|---|---|---|---|---|---|---|---|---|---|---|
| T | F | T | F | T | | T | F | T | F | T |
| T | F | F | T | T | | F | T | F | F | T |
| F | T | T | F | F | | T | F | T | T | F |
| F | T | F | T | T | | T | T | F | T | F |

What happens in the center column? Does the answer surprise you? It shouldn't. After all, either it's Tuesday or it isn't, no matter who's talking about it and no matter when he says it.

If you would like to have a computer to solve your logic problems for you, you can make a simple one this way. First get yourself some 3″ x 5″ index cards, a hole punch (the larger the better) and a long finishing nail or knitting needle. (If your hole punch makes holes large enough for a pencil to slip through, you'll find a pencil more convenient than a nail.)

To start with, take four cards and punch two holes near an edge in all four at once so that the holes on the four cards are exactly lined up. On each of the cards label the first hole *p* and the second hole *q*. Leave the first card exactly as you have it. On the second card, cut out the top of the *q* hole as shown here, but leave the *p* hole alone: On the third card, cut out the *p* hole but leave the *q* hole alone. On the fourth card, cut out both holes. If you use a little imagination, the holes you have cut out look like the number *1* and the holes you have not cut look like zeros. Your four cards can thus be considered to be labeled this way:

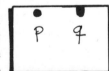

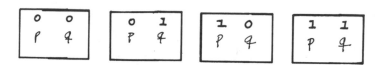

Consider that *1* stands for true and zero for false. (This is easy to remember if you think of zero as nothing, no thing, no, not, not true, and so: false.) The first card thus represents "*p* is false and *q* is false"; the second card shows "*p* is false and *q* is true," and so on.

You can now use your cards to test the question of when *p* ∧ *q* is true. Put the nail through the *p* holes of all the cards. Discard the cards that stay on your tester because these are the cards on which *p* is false. Take the cards that fall off and put your tester through the *q* holes. The card that falls off gives your answer: *p* ∧ *q* is true only when *p* is true and *q* is true, since only the card with both the *p* hole and the *q* hole cut will fall both times.

To test the question of when *p* ∨ *q* is true, put your tester through the *p* holes first. Save the cards that fall for these are *part* of your answer. Take the cards that have not fallen off the tester and put the tester through the *q* hole on these cards. Whatever cards fall off complete your answer. You will see that the only card that does not fall off is the one on which neither hole has been cut; *p* ∨ *q* is true unless *both* *p* and *q* are false.

Since *p* and *q* can stand for any two propositions, your simple computer can be used to check out simple arguments which contain just two propositions. Suppose *p* means, "It is raining" and suppose *q* means "I'll get wet." A very simple argument might be this: "If it is raining, I'll get wet, and it *is* raining." My conclusion is, "I'll get wet." The sentence "If it is raining, I'll get wet," translates into "Either it's not raining, or I'll get wet": ⌐ *p* ∨ *q*. The second premise says $p = T$, $p$ is true. The whole argument is:

$$(\neg p \vee q) \wedge p$$

To check the argument out, first check out $\neg p \vee q$. To check out $\neg p$, put the tester through the $p$ holes and this time save those that stay on because they are the "$p$ is false," the not-$p$ cards. They will be part of the answer. Pick up the cards that have fallen off and put your tester through the $q$ holes. The ones that fall off complete your answer. You now have all the cards on which $p$ is false (and not $p$ is true), *or*, $q$ is true. These are the cards for the first premise. The next part of your argument is $\wedge p$. Put the prong of your tester through the $p$ holes on your first-premise cards. What falls off is your answer. When you look at the one card that falls you will see that it is the one on which $q$ is cut. Cut means "true." The conclusion is "I'll get wet."

With time and patience you can make your computer as complicated as you choose. The more complicated it is, the more complicated the problems it can solve. If you take just four more cards, label and cut them the same way, and then add a third hole on all eight cards labeled $r$, you will be able to solve arguments with premises containing three propositions. Punch a hole for $r$ on all eight cards, lined up together. Leave the $r$ hole alone on your first set of four cards. Cut it out on each of the four cards of the new set. You now have cards that offer all possible combinations of true and false for three propositions:

$$
\begin{array}{cccc}
0\ 0\ 0 & 0\ 1\ 0 & 1\ 0\ 0 & 1\ 1\ 0 \\
0\ 0\ 1 & 0\ 1\ 1 & 1\ 0\ 1 & 1\ 1\ 1
\end{array}
$$

You can now check out a three-part argument like this one:

> If it rains I'll get wet and if I get wet I'll catch a cold, and it's raining, so I'll catch cold.

"If it rains I'll get wet," you'll remember, translates into, $\leftharpoondown p \lor q$. "If I get wet, I'll catch cold" translates into $\leftharpoondown q \lor r$. The whole argument is written:

$$(\leftharpoondown p \lor q) \land (\leftharpoondown q \lor r) \land p$$

Check out $(\leftharpoondown p \lor q)$ just as you did before. You'll have more cards this time, of course. With the cards for your first premise only, check out $(\leftharpoondown q \lor r)$, keeping the cards that stay on the tester when it goes through the $q$ holes and adding to the group any cards that fall off when you put the tester through the $r$ holes. You now have the cards for the first two premises. Now use your tester to find the cards where $p$ is true—the cards that fall off. You will have one card as your answer. It will be the one where $p$, $q$ and $r$ are all cut: it's raining, I got wet, I caught cold.

What conclusion follows from this argument:

> If I don't study, I'll flunk, but if I study I'll miss the ballgame. But I don't want to miss the ballgame.

Translation:

1. If I don't study, I'll flunk = Either I'll study or I'll flunk: $(p \lor q)$
2. If I study, I'll miss the ballgame = Either I won't study or I'll miss the ballgame: $(\leftharpoondown p \lor r)$
3. I don't want to miss the ballgame = I don't miss the ballgame: $\leftharpoondown r$

The whole argument is: $(p \lor q) \land (\leftharpoondown p \lor r) \land \leftharpoondown r$
Can your computer find the conclusion?

If you like the idea of a computer to work your logic problems, you can also make one to check whether the conclusions of categorical syllogisms are valid or to find what premises you need to support proposed conclusions of such syllogisms. Directions for making this computer—a rather more complicated model—will be found in the appendix of this book.

In a real computer, there are some switches which, taken together, are sometimes called the logic section of the computer. The main switches of this group are the AND switch, the OR switch and the NOT switch. There are others, like the IF AND ONLY IF switch, which we shall not discuss here, but which you can find in books about computers.

The AND and OR switches are constructed so that each has two input terminals on which it can receive a pulse, and one output terminal from which it can send a pulse to the next switch. The NOT switch has one input terminal on which it can receive a pulse either from a switch or from another current source, and one output terminal to send a pulse further along the circuit. In the diagrams below an arrow is used to show an incoming or outgoing pulse. A broken line is used to show that no pulse is being received or sent.

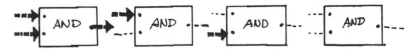

The AND switch will send out a pulse only if it receives a pulse on both input terminals at once.

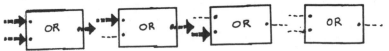

The OR switch will send out a pulse if it receives one on either of its input terminals, or on both.

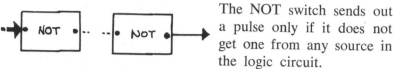

The NOT switch sends out a pulse only if it does not get one from any source in the logic circuit.

If you consider the sending of a pulse to mean "true" and not sending one to mean "false," you can see that the logic section of a computer can easily find the answer to the question of whether $(p \lor \neg q) \lor r$ is true when $p$, $q$ and $r$ are true. As shown in the diagram, since $p$ is true it sends a pulse to the AND switch. A pulse also runs from $q$, since $q$ is true but this pulse goes to the NOT switch because the problem asks for $\neg q$. When the NOT switch receives a pulse it does not send one on, so no pulse goes to the lower input of the AND switch.

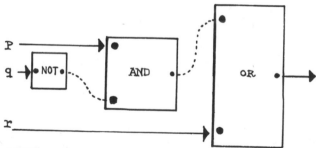

The AND switch therefore sends no pulse to the OR switch. But a pulse from $r$ reaches the OR switch (because $r$ is true) and this is sufficient. The answer is yes. $(p \lor \neg q) \lor r$ is true when $p$, $q$ and $r$ are true.

Probably the light over the stairway in your school can be turned on or off both at the top and at the bottom of the stairs. Or perhaps you have a floodlight on the driveway of your house that can be turned on or off either from the kitchen or the garage. Perhaps you have wired up such

a switch arrangement in science class, using a battery, a
bulb and two double-pole switches in an arrangement like
this:

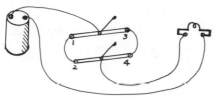

The bulb lights if the switch handles are down at 1 and 2
or at 3 and 4. Otherwise, the light is off. Stated in terms
of symbolic logic: $(p \land \neg q) \lor (\neg p \land q) = T$

The computer's wiring for the so-called "three-way
switch" that operates from two locations would look like
this:

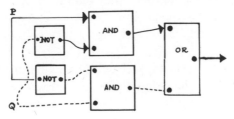

As shown here, the light is lit because $(p \land \neg q) = T$.

And this is really all that the title of this chapter is in-
tended to mean. People argue sometimes about whether a
computer is a thinking machine. It is, to the extent that
thinking consists of dealing with questions that have been
presented before and furnishing answers that are a collec-
tion and sifting of previous answers. It is a very useful
machine for reaching answers to such questions as what is
127 to the 64th power, a tedious question for a person to
have to work out with pencil and paper. It does well in
any situation where there are only two possible choices at

any stage of the reasoning. A computer works best with numbers and it translates every question it gets into terms of numbers. If you look back at your *p-q-r* model for solving logical problems, you will notice that your cards were punched 00,01,10,11,100. . ., the numbers from one to eight in base two, or binary arithmetic. A very large proportion of the computers now in service work on this system.

With this essentially simple system, a computer, working at lightning speed (well, almost) can perform an enormous amount of work. The computer has obvious uses in mathematical computation. It can, for example, check which numbers are prime, by actually trying to divide each number by every other smaller prime. Would you care to discover whether the number 4,294,967,297 is divisible by any number other than itself and one? Would you be a little weary by the time you reached the task of dividing it by 641? The computer works very fast and never gets bored.

Because of its speed and agility in organizing information and performing calculations, a computer can make and keep track of airline reservations, company payrolls, school schedules and bus routes, phone calls and the billing for them. It can handle the mail, direct traffic, predict the result of elections, track satellites, collect medical information to help a doctor in his diagnosis, do library research by selecting, for example, all the legal decisions on a particular subject. It can do an amazing variety of chores for business and industry, even to the point of running a factory.

The thermostat in your house is a simple example of the logic section of a computer at work. It records the temperature in the room. If it is 70° or above, it does nothing. If it is below 70°, it sends out an impulse which turns the furnace on. It continues to record the temperature. When 70° is reached, it turns the furnace off again.

At each stage, the computer chooses one of two possible answers: yes or no, on or off, do this or fail to do it. It handles such choices rapidly and accurately. That is why it succeeds so admirably in working out the correct solution from a set of premises.

Have you ever been stumped by a logical puzzle such as this one?

> The school newspaper reporter reported the following:
> > Bob Zane and the quarterback are friends.
> > Jack Jones and the quarterback are friends.
> > Both Bob and Sam Soho are friends of the student council president.
> > Both the chess champion and the council president are friends of Jack's.
> > Bob, Jack and Sam are all friends.
> Unfortunately, the school reporter was very inaccurate. Two and only two of the statements above are true.

Can you identify the chess champion, the quarterback, and the student council president if you're told that Bob, Jack and Sam is each one of the three?

This is a particularly tough problem of its kind, but a computer, properly programmed, could check it out in seconds. It would discover easily that the first and second sentences can't both be true because, if they were, the last sentence would be true as well, and this is impossible because only two sentences are true. It would then go on to check out every possible pair of sentences. You may tire at the job; it would not.

The computer is quick and thorough at logical reasoning. But logic will not turn on the floodlight of imagination, nor will it light the light of truth.

Please take one more look at your truth table or your computer cards and notice that *any* proposition, true or false, implies a true proposition. If $p$ is either true or false, and if $q$ is true, then "If $p$, then $q$" is true. Symbolically: $(p \lor q)\ q = T$

If jello is the square root of Tuesday, then $2 + 2 = 4$. True, isn't it? But for other kinds of truth we will have to look elsewhere.

# 7

# *The Square Root*
# *of Tuesday*

❂

The search for truth is not a hunt for Easter eggs that someone has hidden for you to find. Yet this is the only kind of truth the computer can furnish, because it cannot use any facts that have not been fed into it, nor can it operate under any rules which are not part of its program.

Before we sent men out to land on the moon, there was a good deal of discussion as to whether the flight should not instead be made by a programmed computer-robot. Then there would be no risk of fatigue, no problems of the effects of weightlessness, no danger to human life. The decision was made to send men, not computers, because a computer can do only what it has been programmed to do, can observe only what it has been programmed to observe and could in no way report on anything except by answering questions that had previously been asked. It cannot be programmed to deal with the wholly unexpected.

If you program the computer with the rules of logic, it will use them to give you logical answers to your questions, but whether the answers make sense or not depends on what you have told the computer about the choice of premises. "If jello is the square root of Tuesday, then $2 + 2 = 4$" makes no more sense—but no less, either—than, "Bishops always travel on the diagonal and no king can threaten another king." Chessplayers will recognize the last sentence as a true and sensible one, *within the rules of chess*. But how is the computer to know the sentence isn't generally true? How about, "If you're out, you're not safe"? The truth of this is obvious—in baseball—but is hardly a general rule of life. You know this, of course, and you have no difficulty in deciding what is meant by "pitcher," "batter," "plate" and "fly" when the words are used by a baseball enthusiast and when they're used by a cook. But a computer will not understand this distinction unless it has been programmed to do so. And it is extremely complicated to program a computer not to make errors of this kind, because the programmer has to think up in advance all the mistakes a computer might possibly make and then program it to avoid them.

Even when you ask a computer to do what it does best— give logical answers to questions—it is still entirely dependent on the premises that have been fed into it. It cannot check on the truth of them. As you have seen, a valid conclusion isn't necessarily true and an invalid one isn't necessarily false. If your premises are true and your argument is valid, then your conclusion is true. If your premises are false and your argument is valid, your conclusion is false. But it's perfectly possible to have an invalid argument with a true conclusion. Perhaps it's easiest to see this with some examples from arithmetic:

If $7 = 5 + 2$, then $7 - 5 = 2$—true premises, valid argument, true conclusion.

If $7 = 4 + 6$, then $7 - 4 = 6$—false premises, valid argument, false conclusion.

If $7 = 4 + 6$, then $7 - 4 = 3$—false premise, invalid argument, true
conclusion.

If I bought a pack of gum for 5¢ and if I gave the store-
keeper a quarter, then I got 20¢ change. The arithmetic is
done correctly. The proof is valid: $25 - 5 = 20$. But if in
fact it was a dime, not a quarter, that I gave to the store-
keeper, then it's not true that I got 20¢ change. The computer could not check on the truth of the premise.

Logical proof, like mathematical proof, can operate on
rigid rules with on-off, true-false, yes-no answers for the
very reason that truth and reality are unimportant to logical
and mathematical proof. In mathematics, you can say $a \times b = b \times a$ with no concern at all for what $a$ and $b$ stand
for. Tell this to a computer and tell it further that $a =$ cats,
$b = $ *rats* and $x = $ *eat,* and it will tell you that cats eat rats
is the same as rats eat cats.

A great deal has been written lately about the value of
computers in education, and quite a few experimental
schools have tried to employ computers as aids to the teach-
ing staff. The claim is made that computer-teaching provides a way of giving students more individual attention
than any teacher in an ordinary classroom situation can
possibly give. Each student, it is argued, can proceed at his
own pace. He will always know immediately whether he is
right or wrong. If his answer is wrong, the computer will
take him through the program again, perhaps by a different
path, until he comes up with the right answer. Then and
only then does the student go on to more difficult material.
He will not be asked to learn a new process until he has
mastered the old. But what does the student "master"?

Let's go through an imaginary program. You are supposed to fill the blanks. In a real situation, the computer

would tell you whether you had filled them correctly, but in this case it would be an insult to your intelligence to suggest you need anyone or any thing to correct your work. Try it:

$2 \times 2 = 4$

$2^2 = 4$. Read this: "The *square* of 2 is 4."

$2^2 = 2 \times$ —

$2^2 = $ — $\times 2$

$2$ — $= 4$

$2^2 = $ —

The square of 2 is —.

$3 \times 3 = 9$

$3^2 = 9$

$3^2 = 3 \times$ —

$3^2 = $ — $\times 3$

$3 \times 3 = 3$ —

The square of — is 9.

$4^2 = $ — $\times$ —

The square of 4 is —.

$16 = 4$ —

$5^2 = $ ———

$n$ — $= n \times n$

$n^2$ means the ——— of $n$, or $n \times$ —.

The *square root* of $n^2$ is $n$.

The square root of 9 is 3.

The ——— root of 16 is 4.

The square ——— of 25 is 5.

$\sqrt[2]{16} = 4$ is the way of writing "the square root of 16 is 4."

$\sqrt[2]{9} = 3$ means "the ——————— of 9 is 3."

$5 \times 5 = 5$ — and $\sqrt[2]{5^2} = $ —.

$5^2 = 25$ and $\sqrt[2]{25} = $ —.

25 is the ——————— of 5, and 5 is the ——————— of 25.

$n^2$ is the square of _____, and $n$ is the _____
   of $n^2$.
If $a \times a = b$, then $a = \sqrt[2]{b}$.
If $a \times a = b$, then $a$ is the _____ of $b$.
If jello $\times$ jello $=$ Tuesday, then the _____
   of Tuesday is jello.
$\sqrt[2]{\text{Tuesday}} =$ _____.
What is the square root of Tuesday? _____

Fine. You passed. Now, doubtless, you're ready to find the square root of Wednesday and pretty soon you can tackle the fourth root of Thursday. Is anything wrong?

Computer programs are fine for learning skills in such areas as arithmetic and spelling. You can learn the symbols for chemical elements and their place on the periodic table. You can learn word equivalents in foreign languages. Programmed learning is mainly useful to make sure that you have read a page and can repeat it. It cannot make sure that you have understood it. It cannot answer any questions you may have about the material and it certainly cannot undertake to argue with you about the answers. (What does "jello $\times$ jello" *mean?* You don't have to know that. Stop fooling around and get on with your work.) You can get the right answers without understanding what you're doing and you can, with equal ease, be marked wrong for a right answer that doesn't happen to match the answer that has been programmed into the computer.

Since any answer you give will be marked wrong unless it is the one that has been programmed into the computer, the question had better be one that has only one right answer. To what extent are you willing to have a computer grade your paper on a test that asks such questions as, "What was the main cause of the Civil War?" or, "What is the best method of town government?"

A computer does an excellent job of compiling information and sorting it out. It can help in the process of *inductive reasoning*—the process of discovering a general rule by examining a number of examples. Up till now we have been involved with *deductive reasoning*—finding what conclusions can correctly be drawn from premises, conclusions that are true if the premises are true. Inductive conclusions can seldom be "true" in this sense, since a perfect inductive conclusion can be made only when *all* examples have been examined, and this is seldom possible. Still, if all the examples you look at support your conclusion and you find none that are exceptions to your rule, you may feel fairly certain that your inductive conclusion is correct. There is no right answer to the question of how many confirming examples are needed. You have a theory that wooden things burn. You test three wooden things: a ruler, a board, a chair. They do burn. Is your inductive conclusion correct? You have another theory that red things are liquid. You examine three of them: cherry soda, wine, and blood. They are liquid. Is your conclusion correct?

People who jump to conclusions often fall flat on their faces. They find a few confirming examples for their conclusions. Then they either stop looking or deliberately look away from any examples that might cast doubt on their conclusions. "Teen-agers are irresponsible drivers." Based on how many examples? "Mexicans are lazy," "Scotchmen are stingy," and all the other national and racial stereotypes are right in a class with the conclusion that all red things are liquid.

But even if an inductive conclusion doesn't state a truth about all members of a class it may be probable to *some* degree. What percentage of teen-agers are irresponsible drivers? The computer can help to find the answer by receiving and sorting all the information you can gather about the driving records of teen-agers and tell you how likely it is that your conclusion is correct, that is, what percent of teen-age drivers are irresponsible. But it depends upon the programmer to give it all the information it needs.

A recent survey was made of the number of turtles inhabiting Lake Titicaca, the world's highest navigable lake, between Peru and Bolivia. Since the area of the lake is over 3,000 square miles, a shell-to-shell census would not be very practical. What the underwater scientists did was to fence off a one-acre section of the lake and to count all the turtles they found in that acre and then to project the figure over the total acreage of the lake. What would one have to know about turtles in Lake Titicaca to have confidence in the reported population figures? Suppose a count were made of the number of people found in an acre of downtown Chicago in a given period of time. Could you estimate the population of the United States by multiplying that number by the acreage of the United States? The computer will perform the same operation to answer both these population questions, because it cannot make value judgments about whether the information it's been given is fairly and sensibly selected.

Opinion polls of all kinds are conducted in much this way. A sample of the population is selected, questions asked, and answers recorded. The computer can then tell what percentage of the people who were questioned held one opinion or another. You would like to know whether Folk-Rock is well liked in the United States. Stop 100,000 people at random at the intersection of the busiest streets in each of ten cities and ask their opinion. Good idea? Would the answer depend at all on whether the questions were asked at 10 A.M. on a school day or at 10 A.M. on Saturday? You know it would, but the computer wouldn't even be able to ask.

People who have faith in computers tend to assign to

them many jobs that are far beyond their capacities. Computers are allowed to screen applicants for jobs, even to weed out people who are already employed. Computers decide who should be allowed to borrow money and who can be trusted with a charge account. Computers have put the old matchmakers and dating bureaus out of business, substituting a computer dating service which will provide you with the names of a handful of suitable people, based on questionnaires you and they fill out. You are asked to describe your age, height, weight and general appearance and those of the person you'd like to date. You are also asked to mark as "True," "False," or "Undecided" such statements as, "Our government should provide more aid to the poor," and, "Romance is important to a marriage," and then to decide whether it is "Unimportant," "Slightly important," "Important" or "Very important" to you that your date shares your views on ten such issues. The computer is efficient. It can work out a problem like this of matching answers to questionnaires. Does this really work to bring the right people together? You might try a simple experiment to find out. If you're going steady, ask your date to make out a questionaire in duplicate with twenty-five or fifty questions he or she considers important. You make one too, on your own. Then match up your *questions*. How many questions appear in both questionnaires? This may turn out to be more important than whether your answers match. Would a dating-bureau computer have brought you two together? And if it wouldn't have, are you about to split?

To what extent do you want a computer to make decisions for you, for the public at large? They are fast, they are efficient and they can even be programmed to learn from their own mistakes and to do better next time. Computers have been programmed to play fairly good games of chess. In 1966–7 there was an international chess match of four simultaneous games between U.S. and Soviet computers. (Just for the record, the Soviets won two and drew— that is, tied—the other two.) In the experiment, the computers' memories were supplied with the rules of chess, the values of the pieces and the different positions on the board. The Soviet computer was programmed to look ahead eight possible moves of its own and eight of its opponent's before deciding on a move. The games took over a year. The machines were programmed only with the best of a variety of moves. A Russian chessplayer who commented on the program said that if the computer had been programmed to consider *all* possible variations for fifteen or twenty moves ahead and if it were able to study *all* possible answers to every move made by its opponent, any one move would take billions of years.

It takes a computer a while to figure out all the possible choices but, given the time, it can do it, and given the proper learning program it can improve. But chess is a game. There are certain fixed rules to be followed, and all you ask of the computer is that it should win according to these rules. When the computer decides to "sacrifice" a knight—that is, to allow one of its pieces to be captured by the other side in order to improve its position, no blood is shed in the "sacrifice." Suppose the "knight" to be sacrificed were a soldier? A battalion of soldiers? Kurt Vonnegut, in a short story called "All the King's Horses" (in *Welcome to the Monkey House,* Delacorte Press, 1968), imagined a situation in which the chess pieces on one side of the board were all people who, when "sacrificed," were killed. Would that make a difference in the strategy of the chessplayer? Should it? How would you program the computer to play that game?

As you have seen, a computer works best with numbers and it translates every question it gets into terms of numbers. The danger lies in the fact that there are quite a few questions which can't be answered in terms of numbers, where the values are not measurable as quantities.

$$\square \times \text{robins} = \triangle \times \text{pounds of fungus-free seed}$$

What numbers will you fit into the box and the triangle to solve this equation? Is it silly? This is the kind of question a computer is asked to answer when it recommends a pesticide to prevent the destruction of seed by fungus and the pesticide is one known to kill robins.

If you program a computer to find the most economical method of manufacturing an item and marketing it, how much do you tell it about whether you want to use shoddy materials, underpaid workers, misleading advertising?

The question is not whether a computer can arrive at logical conclusions or make decisions. Of course it can. The question is rather whether you want to accept the decisions it makes. It has no conscience, no sense of values, and it does not know, unless you tell it, what considerations are important to you. A decision made by a board of education in a large city sounds like one a computer came up with: There had been a great deal of vandalism in the schools. Many windows had been broken by stones thrown by the vandals and the cost to the city of replacing the windows was a heavy expense. The solution? Build schools without windows. The wise men of Gotham could have done no better.

Some people say that they do not trust computers. What they really mean, of course, is that they do not trust the people who decide how they should be programmed, what problems should be entrusted to computers for solution and what guidelines the computer is to use in arriving at a solution. It is people, not computers, who decide to try to destroy insect pests even though the DDT that's used finds its way into the milk that every baby drinks. The computer merely helps to gather the facts, to provide the correct formula for pesticides.

A computer can find, if it is correctly programmed, all the people in an area who are suffering from arthritis. It is not the computer, though, that makes the decision to try to sell these people a so-called cure which will not cure anything. It is people, not computers, who realize that sick people will buy anything that anybody says will cure them, because they are desperate. It is people who program the computers to type out the names and addresses and mail out the advertisements.

The computer is an obedient and tireless servant. It is not good or bad, any more than an axe is good or bad. Whether it builds or destroys depends upon the user. But if you put an axe on automatic, don't be surprised if you come back and find the forest gone, and perhaps the lumberjacks, too.

A computer will answer whatever question you ask of it but it will not decide whether you have asked the right question. It will give you what you ask for, not necessarily what you want. And as for the hidden easter eggs, if you have not encoded the proper messages for the treasure hunt, the computer will not find even these.

# 8

# *Reddi-Think*

A good deal of what passes for decision-making is really a process of finding reasons to support what you know you're going to do. Having decided on a course of action, a person seeks to rationalize, that is, to explain and justify the behavior in a way that at least *seems* reasonable. Sometimes the rationalizing is done so that other people will find your behavior acceptable; sometimes it's done to persuade yourself that you're doing the right thing, even when you're fairly sure you're not.

"I'm only borrowing the glove," says Pete as he opens Stan's locker. "If he were here, I know he'd lend it to me."

"I need this money for a class ring," says Helen to herself as she opens her mother's pocketbook. "If Mother only understood how badly I want the ring, she'd give me the money, but somehow I just can't seem to get through to her."

"I have not knowingly broken any rules," says a New York City policeman. "I'm just challenging their interpretation."

The army has abandoned the use of chemical and biological warfare, as the President instructed it to do. All the army does now is to work through its Military Assistance Program to train people from other countries to use gas and germ weapons but "we do not solicit participation in these training courses," says an army spokesman.

The South African policy of apartheid has been misunderstood, according to its supporters. "Segregation of the races is merely an incidental aspect of the policy. That is why it is being renamed 'multinational development.' We don't discriminate," says the Minister of Administration and Development. "We only recognize the natural differences between people."

An understanding of the rules of logic provides excellent training for rationalizing your way out of many unpleasant situations. Build an argument backwards, start with the conclusion you want to reach and find the premises—*any* premises—that will support it. This, of course, is how to win an argument, to persuade someone to accept the decision you've reached.

As for your opponent's conclusion, there are at least five ways to escape it:

You can attack the premises, saying that the facts are untrue or the assumptions are unreal or, in any event, that the premises are unacceptable to you.

You can accept the premises but point out that the reasoning by which those premises are said to lead to the conclusion is invalid.

You can state your own contrary conclusion and hope to get your opponent to accept your premises and the reasoning which follows from them. To do this, you may have to use an *ad hominem* argument, not because you cannot build a sound argument on true premises, with valid reasoning, but because your opponent is unable to *hear* your argument. Rules when rigidly applied, for example, can be stupid in the extreme. But you had better not try to prove this to the enforcer of the rules. If he believed your argument, he might be led to conclude that his job was of no importance. If the rules he's enforcing are proved to be stupid, then he has a stupid job and is a person of no value. Since he wants to be a valuable, significant person exercising authority in a good cause, he cannot allow you to destroy this self-image. Don't try. Tell him, rather, how important a job he has, controlling the lives of others, what a great deal of responsibility and good judgment is needed to carry out such a job properly. Only a man with humanity, integrity and wisdom, a man such as he is, could handle so delicate a responsibility where there is a constant need to balance the demands of the regulations against the needs of the individual, and to come up with a decision that is fair to all. It isn't everyone, you must assure him, who could be entrusted with such a task. By then, he may be able to hear the reasons why you should be allowed an exception to the rule, where the exception benefits you and hurts no one else.

If your conclusion rests on wobbly premises, or the reasoning is unsound, you can try to persuade your opponent that everybody who is anybody agrees with you. You can rely on authority—"four out of five of the dentists surveyed recommend sugarless gum to their patients who chew gum" —and if you're quick and eloquent you won't have to say just whom or how many you've surveyed. "Simon says, 'Do this!'"

If you can do none of these things, you can use the *ad hominem* argument the other way: attacking the supporter of the argument and showing that, since this fellow is always in the wrong, here is just one more instance of how wrong he is.

As a last resort, you can change the subject and try to do it in such a way that no one will notice you've changed it. Is it impossible to muster enough votes against the resolution that has been proposed and have all the good arguments been used to no avail? Argue that the motion was not properly made and seconded, or that it is out of order, or that not enough members are present, or that the meeting has gone on beyond its scheduled closing time. Is it difficult to show that the accused is innocent? Then his attorney should argue that the jury was unfairly selected or that the case belongs properly in another court. Is the problem of the American Indian that he lacks adequate roads, decent housing, sufficient schools, and job opportunities, and is the Bureau of Indian Affairs unwilling to confront these problems? The way out is to assure the Indian's representative that the important question to resolve is the relation between primitive and advanced civilizations. And this, it is clear, is the task of the anthropologists, not that of the Bureau.

This is how arguments are won. Perhaps the book should end here. It is a book about how to construct an argument and how to break one down, regardless of what that argument is. It is a book about logic, not truth. It is a book about thinking straight and learning to recognize when the thinking is crooked. But if you have come this far, perhaps you will be willing to consider one more question: what is the purpose of thinking and what sort of problems require decisions? Is it the goal of thinking to put as many things as possible into proper pigeonholes, finding as many answers as you can, and storing them away for ready reference? If it is, the computer will outwit and outlast you. It can scan research material and store the needed information in capsule form with greater speed and far better memory than you will ever achieve. It can sort material into the proper pigeonholes and bring it out again on command.

What is man for and what are machines for? If the answer to both questions is the same—for the efficient running of a complex civilization—then the machine will win over man any day now, for the machine is already more efficient than man in many areas and is daily entering and winning the competition in more and more fields of human endeavor. But if the answers to the two questions are different, then it is important to stop and consider what these differences are, to decide what we do and do not want the machines to do for us. Are we tired of thinking? of making decisions? of assuming responsibility? of creating? of making judgments about what we like, about what we think is right or beautiful or worthwhile? Do we want the machines not only to do our work but also to do our playing for us, to direct our leisure time? The machine can do almost anything we ask of it.

You don't have to whip cream any more. You can just squirt it out of a can under pressure. Of course, what comes out of the can isn't cream. It doesn't taste very much like cream, but it *looks* like it and it saves so much time and trouble and hardly ever goes sour.

Our Western civilization today is built around labor-saving devices of all kinds. From TV dinners to packaged kits ready to assemble we have all but outlawed the pleasure people used to take in working with their hands and making something truly their own. We save time by a myriad of labor-saving devices, but it is not entirely clear what we propose to do with the time we save.

Do you enjoy fishing? It's a terribly inefficient method of extracting food from the environment. Walking? You enjoy walking! Why, that's how the caveman got around. Think how civilization has advanced since then. Aren't you going to take advantage of the means of transportation your civilization provides for you?

Do you want the machine to do your reading for you? The newspaper, for instance. Reading it takes a lot of time. Would you rather have the machine give you a brief report on what has taken place and what you should think about what has taken place? Do you want the machine to make your decisions for you? The time is not so far off when it will be able to, if you let it.

Of course, you want it to do some of your routine work, whether it's thinking, or washing clothes, or getting you from here to there. For some of this kind of thinking, man himself goes "on automatic," and must, to survive. Habit frees a person from the need to figure out routine things. Which arm shall you put first into your coat, the left or the right? Happily you don't have to answer this question in order to get your coat on. Whichever way you do it, that is the way to do it. One of the big advantages of learning and practice in arithmetic is that you do not have to stop and think what nine and five are. You get an automatic answer when you ask yourself the question. In fact, if you do stop and think about routine matters, you may actually slow down or even entirely inhibit their accomplishment. A good typist knows perfectly well where each letter of the keyboard is, as long as the typing is going on. But ask him to stop and tell you exactly where the *g* is, or the *n,* or the *c,* and he may be, for the moment, stymied.

The need for thinking arises when something goes wrong with the routine, and not until then, or when a new situation comes up for which you have not yet established any routine. A young child is faced with a great many such problems. For him, tying shoelaces is a really difficult affair. If you want to remember just how difficult it was, try to teach a child to do it. Can you remember what a problem it was to decide which shoe belonged on which foot?

The child adding nine and five must either count on his fingers, or add one to make ten, or go through some other laborious rigmarole until the time when he can automatically answer "fourteen." The experience of doing the same thing over and over and over and over develops habit patterns that enable you to put yourself on automatic and do no thinking about the subject at all. If all of a person's training in school has been the establishment of patterns and the developing of the ability to react quickly to such questions as what is nine and five, or what is the capital of Honduras, or when was the Dominion of Canada established, he may find himself having neither the need nor any longer even the capacity to cope with new problems. He looks for answers in the simplest and quickest form in which he can find them. He prefers his meals precooked, his news predigested, his opinions already formulated for him in the editorials of his favorite paper or weekly news magazine.

These are the people who, even in their leisure time prefer to find the answers ready-made. They like to paint in the paint-by-number boxes; they like to use crossword puzzle dictionaries; they especially like to find the answers to questions at the end of the chapter. They are the people most seriously disturbed when a detour sign blocks their usual way of traveling, because they have always traveled the same route, once they found the fastest and most efficient way of getting somewhere. These are the people who are most distressed when the brand they have been buying disappears from the grocer's shelf. They are the ones least able to understand that other people may not think exactly as they do, behave exactly as they think proper, have the same habits of eating and dressing, the same tastes in entertainment. Their habits, their patterns, their opinions have become routinized to the point where there is nothing left to think about. It is *the way* they do something; it is, it must be, the way everybody does it. They vote for a particular party because they have always voted for that party, perhaps even because their parents have voted in this way, and their parents before them. There are no issues to consider because they have all been long resolved by authority.

It is against the routine-bound existence that protests occur in student groups. It is because life is just too much of an unthinking, reflex action, where no decisions are called for or even possible to make, that violent changes in habits of dress and behavior catch on. "I shall not automatically shave," the young man thinks. "I can wear a beard if I like. I will not have my hair cut every third Saturday. I will let it grow to shoulder length if I choose."

"I shall have a variety of clothes to choose from," says the girl. "Monday, I will wear a miniskirt. Tuesday? Perhaps pants. Wednesday, if I feel like it, a maxi coat. I have five shades of eye shadow. I can change the color of my hair. I can wear a wig. I need not know from one minute to the next what I will look like, what I will wear. For I will not be set into a mold. You will not pigeonhole me."

What this is, or may be saying, is a larger statement: I do not want to be in the mold you have put me in. I do not want to be in any mold, but there's not much I can do to get out of the mold of the society in which I live. I cannot change the fact that when the alarm rings I get up, I walk to the corner where I catch the bus for school, I go to my homeroom, I follow a schedule you have arranged for me, I come home, I do the household chores that are expected of me, I do my homework, I go to bed at the appointed hour. These things I cannot change, though I would like to. It is not so much that I dislike what it is I have to do as that I dislike the fact that there is a pattern to it which allows of no thought and no decision-making. So I will make decisions about those things I *can* make decisions about. If I have any free time, I will use it to play the music I like. (And so much the better if the authority figures dislike it.) And I will play it loud and strong so you will know I have made this choice. And the choices I make in clothing and makeup, in beads and buttons, in speech and behavior, will be loud enough, startling enough and strange enough so that you will know that there is a person there, not a cog, not a unit in an overall pattern like the leaf repeated on the wallpaper. You will know there is someone inside, a decision-maker.

You program my life at home, in school, in camp. You tell me what I may not drink, or smoke, what movies I may not look at. You tell me I may not vote, or participate even remotely in the decision-making process. In a little while you will program me into a uniform, an army camp, a war. And about all this I have no choice offered. So I make decisions where I can.

As a banner, an emblem, a symbol, the long hair and the bizarre costumes, the beads and the buttons are fine. But symbols, to be useful, must symbolize something. The protest against the routinizing of life must, to make any sense, be a protest against those aspects of life that ought not to be routine. Otherwise, one might just as well protest by saying, "I've always stuck my left arm first into my coat sleeve; I shall begin to stick my right arm in first. I have always brushed my teeth up and down; I'll start to brush them from side to side."

People who create problems for themselves as to what to wear on a given day or how long their hair should be, are saying, in effect, there are no real problems to deal with so we will have to create some in order to be able to make some decisions of our own. They are not too different a breed from the people in last year's news who sought recognition by claiming a world record for the longest kiss— one hour, thirty-five minutes and forty seconds—or for swallowing 225 goldfish in forty-two minutes. Their protests are hardly more significant than those of the college students in India who demanded the right to cheat on exams.

Is it true that there are no real problems? Does it comfort you to learn from the newspaper that should there be a nuclear attack against the United States, it will not mean the end of the world, at least not for New Yorkers? There's a fallout bunker kept in constant readiness. It will house 700 state officials and the fourteen people needed for house-keeping chores. The bunker is stacked with instant soup in six flavors: beef noodle, mushroom, onion, potato, chicken rice, and chicken noodle. The newspaper didn't mention it but, perhaps, for extra flavor, there's a topping of Reddi-think, and the square root of Tuesday for dessert.

# Do You Want
# to Go Deeper?

If you feel you've just gotten your feet wet in logic and the water feels good and you'd like to swim, you might try any of the following:

*Clear Thinking* by Hy Ruchlis. (Harper & Row, 1962.)

*The Art of Making Sense* by Lionel Ruby. (Lippincott, Keystone paperback, 1954.)

*New Puzzles in Logical Deduction* by George J. Summers. (Dover Publication, paperback, 1968.)

*101 Puzzles in Thought and Logic* by C. R. Wylie. (Dover Publication, paperback, 1957.)

*The Story of Computers* by Roger Piper. (Harcourt Brace, 1964.)

*Alice Through the Looking Glass* by Lewis Carroll. (No, it's not a baby book—unless you happen to be a baby.)

Any of the Sherlock Holmes stories, by A. Conan Doyle. They all present fine examples of logical deduction.

The game of WFF 'N PROOF, *The Game of Modern Logic,* by Layman E. Allen.

# Appendix

## *How to Make a Syllogism Computer*

You will need sixteen index cards (and you'd better have a few extra around in case you make mistakes), a hole-punch and two long finishing nails or knitting needles.

Punch sixteen holes in exactly the same position on all sixteen cards in this form:

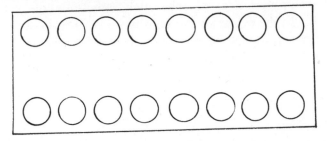

The first card is your premise card. Each hole stands for a possible premise, and there are only sixteen possible premises for categorical syllogisms. To label the holes call the subject of your conclusion *S*. Call the predicate *P* and call the middle term *M*. Thus in the syllogism

> All birds have wings.
> Some birds can't fly.

Therefore    Some creatures with wings can't fly.

The premises are "All *M* are *S*" and "Some *M* are not *P*."

The conclusion is "Some *S* are not *P*."
These are the labels for the eight holes at the top of the card:

 1. All *M* is *P*   2. All *P* is *M*   3. All *S* is *M*   4. All
 *M* is *S*   5. Some *M* is *P*   6. Some *P* is *M*   7. Some
 *S* is *M*   8. Some *M* is *S*

These are the labels for the 8 holes at the bottom of the card:

 1. No *M* is *P*   2. No *P* is *M*   3. No *S* is *M*   4. No
 *M* is *S*   5. Some *M* is $\widetilde{P}$   6. Some *P* is $\widetilde{M}$   7. Some
 *S* is $\widetilde{M}$   8. Some *M* is $\widetilde{S}$   ($\widetilde{P}$ = not *P*)

The other fifteen cards are your conclusion cards, because
there are fifteen possible combinations of premises that will
produce a valid conclusion.

   To make the conclusion card for the syllogism about
birds with wings label the fourth top hole "All *M* is *S*" to
match your premise card. Label the fifth bottom hole "Some
*M* is $\widetilde{P}$." In the center of the card write "Conclusion: Some
*M* are not *P*." Then cut the two holes you've labeled. Your
conclusion card looks like this:

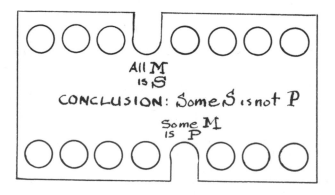

Directions for the fifteen conclusion cards will be given at the end.

To work your computer, line up all fifteen conclusion cards behind the premise card. Stick your nail or needle through the hole for your first premise. Some cards will fall off. Start again, lining up the cards that fell off behind your premise card and sticking your nail or needle through the second premise. Only one card will fall off and it will be your correct conclusion card. (If both premises are on the top, you can save time by putting two nails through at once, one through each premise hole. Only one card will fall and it will be the correct conclusion card.) If no cards fall, there is no valid conclusion based on your premises.

To use your computer to build an argument when all you know is the conclusion you want, sort your conclusion cards (directions below) to pick out only those which have the conclusion you're looking for. Then, by looking at which premise holes are punched on these cards, you can discover what proof you need to build your argument.

If this seems like much more work than it's worth, don't plan on computer programming as a career. After all, a computer cannot give out any answers that have not been programmed into it and getting the answers in *is* work. You can always use your head and a pencil to draw Venn diagrams.

These are your fifteen conclusion cards:

| Conclusion | Premise holes to label and cut | |
|---|---|---|
| 1. All $S$ is $P$ | All $M$ is $P$ | All $S$ is $M$ |
| 2. Some $S$ is $P$ | All $M$ is $P$ | Some $S$ is $M$ |
| 3. Some $S$ is $P$ | All $M$ is $P$ | Some $M$ is $S$ |
| 4. Some $S$ is $P$ | All $M$ is $S$ | Some $M$ is $P$ |
| 5. Some $S$ is $P$ | All $M$ is $S$ | Some $P$ is $M$ |

|     |                  |                    |               |
|-----|------------------|--------------------|---------------|
|  6. | No $S$ is $P$    | No $M$ is $P$      | All $S$ is $M$ |
|  7. | No $S$ is $P$    | No $P$ is $M$      | All $S$ is $M$ |
|  8. | No $S$ is $P$    | No $S$ is $M$      | All $P$ is $M$ |
|  9. | No $S$ is $P$    | No $M$ is $S$      | All $P$ is $M$ |
| 10. | Some $S$ is not $P$ | Some $S$ is $M$  | No $M$ is $P$ |
| 11. | Some $S$ is not $P$ | Some $S$ is $M$  | No $P$ is $M$ |
| 12. | Some $S$ is not $P$ | Some $M$ is $S$  | No $M$ is $P$ |
| 13. | Some $S$ is not $P$ | Some $M$ is $S$  | No $P$ is $M$ |
| 14. | Some $S$ is not $P$ | Some $S$ is not $M$ | All $P$ is $M$ |
| 15. | Some $S$ is not $P$ | Some $M$ is not $P$ | All $M$ is $S$ |

To sort cards to collect a particular conclusion:

There is only one card with the "All $S$ is $P$" conclusion. Find it by its premises.

To find "No $S$ is $P$," put the nail through all the four right-hand holes on the top and the four right-hand holes on the bottom, one at a time in succession. Those that stay on the nail right through the eight tries are the cards you want.

To find "Some $S$ is $P$," put the nail in succession through all the bottom holes. The cards that stay on are those you want.

To find "Some $S$ is not $P$," collect all the cards that fall off when the nail goes through the bottom eight holes. This will give you "Some $S$ is not $P$" and also "No $S$ is $P$." Remove the latter group by going through the eight holes on the right and saving the cards that fall. (Of course, if you don't want to go to the trouble to be fully computerized, you can pick out the four "No $S$ is $P$" cards by looking at them; it's less work.)

# Index